The Correct Way To Fool Around
Part Two
By Jeremiah Dotson

THE SECOND INSTALLMENT OF THE ULTIMATE CHEATER'S REFERENCE

I0425134

Table Of Contents

ACKNOWLEDGEMENTS

First off, I would like to thank Lolita, Anisha, Sabrina from the Bx, Veronica and Ernestine. These are just a few of the women I've dated who for one, have contributed to extending my belief that many women have what I like to call DEEP ROOTED ISSUES! Women such as these, aside from needing extensive parenting courses, believe that it's okay to delude members of the opposite sex by making them think they are the only ones romantically involved in their life. Women such as these, act the way men have been thought to act for years – like dogs. They just do it so well because they use the guise of stupidity or naiveté to accomplish their deceitful and unfair goals. When I use the term deep rooted issues, I am basically saying that these women involved themselves with me while they were involved with someone one else. Some of these women informed me of this when we first met - which is the type of honesty I like and respect from a person, but some waited until I found out on my own that I was nothing more than sex on the side. Now for those of you who may not know, when you cheat, it's not just to have fun (although some misguided individuals believe that). It's not just because you want a little something - something on the side. It's not even because you feel you have no other options or because you feel you got caught up in the moment. It's because you have issues! Anytime you promise fidelity to someone and at the first sign of trouble, you go and drop your drawers to the first handsome man that approaches, you have some serious need of therapy. Now don't get me wrong because I was definitely a willing participant in some of this but I was never the one who was deceitful or the one already involved with somebody else. So yes, I was the proverbial 'victim' here and my attempt is not so much to discredit these women as much as it is to thwart the attempts of these women to do to anybody else what they have done to me. As with the majority of the books that I write, my main intent is not for people to perform irreparable acts of debauchery but more so for people to become and stay aware of things which may be detrimental to their relationship's existence. I believe that these women mentioned above need to do some serious soul searching, as well as esteem searching before they attempt to involve themselves with anyone else because relationships are not rather never supposed to be initiated on just sex or the promise of unless of course that is what both parties desire. These women are attractive in their own respects but have little else going for them. They have no marketable skills, can barely cook and if they were to read these words, which were written about them, are so dimwitted, they would probably come back and ask 'are you talking about me?' This should kinda give you an idea of the types of women I chose to date as well as the high level of deception there is in this world. I mean truth be told - they fooled me. But I have since learned to look for a relationship based on more than outward appearance and I honestly hope the same for the ones stated above. I won't mention the last names of these women to avoid a potential lawsuit as well as a butt whippin' and I sincerely hope that by the time of this book's printing that these five women above change their ways as have I - but just in case they don't, a warning to men everywhere; if you find yourself interested in women with the above first names, who already have children, to save yourself extensive and possibly irreparable headache as well as heartache, run! – Run like your ass is on fire. Run like there's a pit bull attempting to devour off a piece of your anatomy. Run to save your sanity as well as your heart!

Second, I would like to thank everybody for all of the creative criticism and colorful feedback I received regarding my first book, The Correct Way To Fool Around and my second book; Relationships, Pacification For Crazy People Everything from 'I have a new understanding of the cheating world' to 'I never knew there was so much deception involved in relationships' to 'Your books ain't shit!' has helped me realize that after all these years people are still pretty much in the dark, as well as overly sensitive about the topic of infidelity.

Next, I would like to thank Kathy for everything – from the financial support to the spiritual and emotional; I owe you so much it cannot be expressed through mere words.

You will always be loved!

What would my acknowledgements be without telling at least one Security Company to kiss a certain part of my anatomy? This time around, that honor is reserved for my former employer Copstat security, now known as Andrews International. Pucker up!

And as always, Mark & Corey – I Love You.

In the last part of the acknowledgements section of my first book, The Correct Way To Fool Around, I mentioned how I believed it was 'natural' for a man to be a dog, just as it was 'natural' for a woman to be a bitch. Due to the fact that many people felt I was unfairly dogging men and totally disrespecting women, I feel I must once again clarify that statement. As I explained in chapter eleven of The Correct Way To Fool Around, part one, the 'natural' term was nothing more than another way of expressing how comfortable some people were with committing the act of infidelity. Some people cheat so much, it seems as if it's a 'natural' occurrence – as if it comes 'natural' to them. When I referenced the word dog, meaning men and bitch, meaning the female version of, I was speaking only of the people who cheat on their significant others with no regard for their feelings whatsoever. In that sense, I, as well as many other people, believe the dog and bitch monikers to be more than appropriate. There is another term, which I use quite frequently throughout my books as well. That term is trifling. It means insignificant, trivial or of little value. It applies to men as well as women but above all it applies to those people who don't know they are. It applies to those dogs & female dogs or 'bitches' mentioned above and more importantly, it applies to many of the women I have dealt with before. So for all of you overly sensitive buttholes who did nothing more than read the acknowledgements section of my first book and chose to judge the entire book based on that alone, kiss something!

Chapter One
The Love And Mystery
Of Deception...

THE CORRECT WAY TO FOOL AROUND PART 2

I would like to start this chapter by outlining some of the major weapons used in different types of combat today. This spectrum of weapons can vary greatly, from the massively large to the unbelievably small depending upon what type of confrontation people may be involved in. For instance, in the case of world war, there are the weapons of mass destruction, more commonly known as the 'we have 'em but we just don't want the United States to know we have 'em' nuclear missiles. These weapons are not available to the general public but their sole purpose is to cause as many casualties as humanly possible. Think about it, why else would anyone want to possess these weapons? It's not just to prove a point. It's to dominate. When it comes to skirmishes, which do not require government intervention, there are other types of bombs and or incendiary devices, which while not created to cause millions of deaths worldwide, were created to cause casualties and injuries nonetheless. These can be anything from hand grenades to letter bombs, even Molotov cocktails. Usually when the above types of weapons are employed, they leave little room for retaliation. Think about it; when a person or group just happens to be on the receiving end of a hand grenade, how many times does said person or group walk away? Almost never. And think about those letter bombs or small package bombs - until a few years ago who would have thought that a person or group could have been so ingenious or so treacherous as to manipulate someone's expectations from 'oh joy a letter!' to 'oh shit! 'A bomb!'

Now when it comes to the common street fights, there are readily available guns, which range in size from the assault variety (some capable of dispensing over one hundred bullets a minute) to the basic level, pocket sized revolver, capable of releasing firepower commensurate to how fast one can pull a trigger. Now all of these weapons mentioned above have the capability to do one of two things, either hurt you or kill you. In the previous examples, physical, concrete weapons are used and sometimes from great distances but in face to face combat or in many relationships, a different, abstract weapon is often desired. That weapon is called deception. Deception is arguably one of man's greatest weapons. It is a weapon, which while not equal to those of mass destruction, has the capability to greatly deceive the masses. I find this statement about deception being one of the greatest weapons that man has access to, to be truer, more thought provoking and more overlooked than any I have ever heard. This statement is also the unwritten law by which Government Agents, terrorists and magicians often live by. The meaning of the word deception is not limited to just lying to or betraying someone, it is more an act of trickery intended to make a person or a group of people believe the total opposite of what actually exists. In regards to cheating, deception is as necessary an ingredient as food is to one's existence. Cheating involves secrecy, secrecy involves concealment and concealment of truth and or certain facts is a major part of deception. One of the truly wonderful things about deception is its very nature of perfection. To deceive someone, you must be able to eradicate all possibility of mistakes. Living as part of a committed union with someone for twenty years while they have secretly been in another relationship for ten. Living as a white person when both your parents are light skinned black. Working as an undercover operative in one country, while stealing secrets for another, all methods of deception. Now these may be extreme examples but one of the most simplest and overlooked examples of deception is the 'I'm too good to cheat' belief which many folks try and pass on to others. Now nobody in their right mind would normally believe a statement such as this but what helps this type of deception is the fact that people often try to look for the good in others combined with the fact that many people do not give deception the credit it is due. They feel that they are too smart to be deceived by just anyone. They feel that if there were anyone crafty enough to deceive them, it would have to be none other than the great deceiver himself, Satan. These people do not realize however that a young child, who most would think has nothing but pure intentions and school work on the mind would know how to create mass hysteria by leaving school early without telling anyone and going to an arcade for a few hours or how that same child who may get up in the middle of the night to urinate, could manipulate the feelings of his overprotective parents by pretending to cough loud enough until one of them wakes up and says 'okay mister, you're not going to school tomorrow.' Believing that a person is above doing wrong is

<u>what allows deception to exist.</u> Too many people in relationships reside on what I like to call 'clouds of complacency.' These people believe that as long as they're not arguing, their relationships are good. They don't stop to realize that some folks are experts at holding things in and one of the main reasons people hold things in is because many a violent episode has sprung from someone saying something smart or out of anger. These people also feel that they know their partners so well, they're able to tell what their partners are thinking, feeling and doing or about to do at any given moment. These people do not realize that no one knows anyone that completely. The most people can know about someone is a good portion of that person. That portion may be seventy, eighty or even ninety percent but you will never know one hundred percent of anyone in this world. Reason being, there are many situations in life, which make people act totally out of character. Family issues, desperation and fear will make some people do what others would never think they were capable of. What people need to understand is that almost anyone can be deceived and that almost anyone can be deceived by almost anybody. There's a saying, which goes 'you can learn something from everybody in this world because everybody knows something you don't.' Take heed, because the thing you don't know is often what others will use against you. As mentioned before, cheating is a form of deception. One of the main components of cheating is secrecy. If a person is involved in a relationship and has another sexual

relationship that their partner fully knows about, that is cheating but not as much as it is a partial form of swinging. The only difference with swinging is that both parties in the relationship have 'relations' with both of the parties in another relationship. The operative word here again is secrecy. Secrecy works in conjunction with deception so well because the less a person knows about their partner or their partner's true intentions, the easier it is for that person to be deceived. This can be a doubled edged sword because how can someone truly know another or another's true intentions for that matter? People will always say that when there is true love or true feelings, that the heart will be able to tell. This is little more than wishful thinking in my opinion because as history has and continues to show - the heart is one of the most easily manipulated things in this world. A prime example can be that of an older man manipulating the mind of a younger woman for sex or even a person raised in a small town who moves to a big city and is taken advantage of because they are not aware of the big city games. The previous examples are nothing more than common sense and most people already know or should know to be aware of them. The only problem is that too many people again look for the good in others. These people think that since they were raised correctly or properly, everybody else was raised just as correct and or proper. These people do not realize that there are some people in this world who will hurt you just because they are able to. This is where the saying 'there's a sucker born every minute' comes from. This does not mean to imply that anybody in this world is a quote unquote sucker; it just means to say that some people are too trusting. Now combine that with someone manipulating that trust and you have a wonderful recipe for failure especially in relationships. Some people jump into relationships prematurely and by prematurely, I do not mean two weeks, a month or two months of knowing a person, I mean before the time it takes to become completely secure in the relationship you have with this person. Now I will be the first to admit that deception is strong – so strong sometimes that it may take years before a person realizes that his or her relationship is a fraud. But people need to take time and not just a society specified amount of time as in a person in a relationship must be married within three years otherwise he or she should end the relationship but the amount of time someone needs to feel totally comfortable and secure with said person. Of course there will be butterflies, insecurities and uneasiness in any relationship but when these things rule the relationship as opposed to just being a little bit bothersome, the proceed with caution flag should be raised. People use education and the lack of to take advantage of and deceive others and it's done so much that many will argue that it's human nature to take advantage of the less fortunate, as well as to deceive the less educated. One should understand though, cheating occurs in all walks of life as well as at all educational levels. The only major differences are the methods and the number of infractions. As I mentioned in The

Correct Way To Fool Around, Part One and in my second book; Relationships, Pacification For Crazy People - and as I always tell folks, I am not in any way condoning the act of infidelity nor am I intending to promote promiscuous behavior, I just happen to enjoy discussing controversial subjects and the information within is based on my experiences with people I personally know. Now while almost everybody in this world knows the basics surrounding how it occurs, one cannot honestly talk about infidelity without examining some of the reasons why. In all honest estimation, I believe there are hundreds, maybe even thousands of reasons why a person would choose to be unfaithful to their partners but what quickly comes to mind are the following: Unhappiness, Revenge, Excitement and Lack of Intimacy.

Unhappiness

One of the biggest and most basic reasons I've found people have for cheating, aside from revenge is general unhappiness. Unhappiness can stem from boredom, from getting involved with a partner too quickly or because the relationship is not going the way a person wants it to go and for some reason or another, they feel trapped. Personally, I don't believe anyone gets involved in a relationship with the sole intent of becoming unhappy. I believe people get into relationships because they want to either maintain their present level of happiness or raise it to a higher level with someone else. In any relationship, it's a known fact that people have several responsibilities to one another. Aside from the basic unwritten ones like commitment and fidelity, one, which many always seem to overlook or confuse, is the responsibility of maintenance. By this, I do not mean dealing with particularly high or low maintenance people, I mean everyday people who deserve to be kept at or above the level they were at before you met them. If you as a person in a relationship cannot keep the person you are involved with in a capacity equal to or better than what they had before they met you, you should not be in a relationship with them - and by capacity, I'm not talking about weight restrictions, I'm referring to standard of living. If for instance, you are the type of person who wears a large amount of jewelry and you get involved with someone who has you making monthly trips to the pawnshop because of their inabilities at budgeting, you should not be involved with them. This applies mostly to men because historically, men have had to take care of women and families but women have to bear the load at times too. A woman cannot always act like a queen and have a man suffer as a result. On the same token, a man cannot expect to have a happy and peaceful relationship with a professional woman if he is habitually unemployed. Love is one thing – bankruptcy is definitely another. In addition to the responsibility of maintenance, there is also the responsibility of time. Ample time between a committed couple must be available. A person in a committed relationship will rarely be able to work eighty or ninety hours a week and have enough time and energy to make happy his or her significant other. Even if the person working the excessive number of hours is doing so to keep their mate at a certain level, the mate will often feel neglected and possibly go searching for fulfillment elsewhere. Unhappiness occurs when the two parallel paths a couple is traveling on just happen to go awry. In a relationship, people usually have a certain plan for how they want their lives together to turn out. The woman for instance may desire two kids, life in a quiet town close to her folks, moderate sized home, surrounded by a white picket fence. The man on the other hand may have his heart set on no kids, a big apartment, a European sports car and a large and ferocious, yet pretty white dog. People have their own thoughts, schemes, five-year plans – whatever, which they base their present day decisions on. These decisions are fine and all to the individual party as long as they don't upset the other party's long-term goals. Unhappiness sets in when people start to veer off their chosen paths because of the person they are involved with or when compromise is taken too far. If the woman described above has her heart dead set on kids and her boyfriend or husband has his heart dead set on being forever childless, sooner or later, this issue will cause at least one of them to be unhappy, leading to either an eventual separation or an eventual change. In the hypothetical description above, both the man and the woman desire things, which they believe will eventually make them happy. If they are not both loving and mature enough to relinquish a small part of what their prospective happiness entails, then they will eventually become unhappy together or happy alone. An unhappy relationship can be compared to a job someone is unhappy with. In an unhappy employment position, do most people wait to get fired before looking for a new job? Do these people continue in their unhappy position while allowing their dislike to reflect on their job performance? Or do they start searching, while unhappy, in preparation for the inevitable? The answer is of course to start searching for something new before the inevitable inevitably happens. Now there are many reasons why unhappiness becomes part of a relationship. A few of the more common reasons are lack of communication, the fact that people are not true with their original or actual agendas and because people lose focus on what's really important in the relationship. When it comes to <u>communication</u> or the lack of, many people seem to feel that as long as there are words being spoken, then there is honest and effective communication. The problem here is that in order to communicate effectively, one must not only be able to communicate words but feelings as well. A couple should be able to communicate feelings of happiness as well as the opposite, feelings of trust or distrust and even feelings of insecurity. But what many couples do is say things like 'I don't trust you!' without giving reasons or 'you don't please me anymore' without even attempting to work at the problem. Instead of couples being as open and honest with one another as possible, they hide things. Instead of a married woman saying 'I have to go see my child's father' she will hide it from her husband. Then when the husband finds out, whether through somebody telling him or through his own detective work, the lack of trust will enter the relationship or escalate. Now even if the interaction between the wife and the ex husband is purely on the up and up, the fact that it was hidden will cause unhappiness. Many people will say that since nothing happened there is no reason for the husband to get upset. Maybe not but what if the husband had experienced infidelity in his previous relationship and the circumstances surrounding it or leading to it were eerily similar to what is happening in the present. Again it's the fact that something was being kept away from the significant other - this is lack of communication - this causes distrust - this causes unhappiness. Another thing, which causes a great deal of unhappiness is deception. As stated above, sometimes people are not true to the <u>actual agendas </u>when they get involved in relationships. Some of these people will involve themselves with another just to reap the immediate gratification and temporary benefits of being in a relationship. Now this is not completely wrong because everybody has an agenda when he or she becomes involved with another. The only problem or major problem is that they don't always let the agenda become known to the person they are involved with. Many people in this world do bad things. Many more people are just bad. Some of these bad people take advantage of the fact that others are experiencing desperation. Some single people have been single for so long that they are desperate to have a relationship. Maybe they have never been in a relationship or maybe they have never been happy in any of their previous relationships. Whatever the case, the bad people will use the fact of desperation to manipulate the relationship into what they want it to be. For example, if a person has been single for a long time, the bad person may try and rush the relationship. If the person has never been in a relationship, the bad person will make it appear that he or she is the best one to be in a relationship with and will subsequently make the prospect of being in a relationship with this person seem like the best thing that could ever happen. If the desperate person has never been happy in any of his or her previous relationships, then the bad person will do whatever he or she can to never make the other unhappy and this is done so that the previously unhappy person will think that the bad person is actually good and will subsequently bestow the bad person with any and everything the bad person desires - AKA a fake relationship. This causes temporary happiness up until the bad person either gets enough of whatever it was he or she wanted or until the significant other of the bad person wants something in the form of a more serious commitment which the bad person is not in any way shape or form willing to give. This will result in an attempt at deeper communication, which the bad person will most often try every trick in the book to avoid, which will result in unhappiness on the part of both - the bad person because he or she will no longer be able to get whatever it was that he or she was receiving and the good person because he or she will be left without a relationship. When it comes to <u>losing focus</u> in a relationship, this does not mean that a person cannot see clearly. It means that the partner, AKA the immediate family, who should be the main focus, begins to take a back seat to a myriad of things - for example, the rest of the family and in laws (and this is because we all know parents interfere) and employment and friends and bills, etc. In many relationships, people listen to their parents and even the parents of the significant other about the significant other as opposed to listening to the significant other. This causes a big rift in the communication which is supposed to be between the husband and wife. Far too often people feel that when something is exciting, it is more believable that what may be ordinary truth. If a person has a history of infidelity, it may be easier for someone to convince the significant other of that person that something adulterous may have happened within the relationship than it would be for the significant other to convince the wife or husband of the opposite. I mean who hasn't heard of the famed 'girl, he probably cheating on you - he's a man, that's what they do! And wasn't he cheating on his ex wife with you when yall first met anyway?' I have experienced this scenario countless times, personally and through several acquaintances. This happens mainly because of the communication breakdown or because of the lack of communication to begin with. Other things, which cause unhappiness, include the employment situation. We as human beings have to face one universal fact and that is that no matter how much love there seems to be in a relationship, if there is not a sufficient financial foundation in said relationship to adequately sustain the relationship, the relationship will fail. This does not mean to say that if one party has a million dollars in his or her bank account and the significant other has nothing, meaning no job or resources, the relationship will work - because it won't. Don't misunderstand me, a person can take care of another for a month, a few months or even a few years but eventually the caretaker will become tired. Even though the capability is there for one person to take care of another for life, this is not the thing happy relationships are based on. People have to contribute to the relationship equally. This does not mean that if a person buys you a one thousand dollar suit, you have to run right out and buy that person a one thousand dollar dress. It means that the effort should be rewarded and reciprocated. But here comes a lot of the miscommunication - many mismatched couples feel that 'damn the thought that counts, I bought you something expensive - I want something just as costly!' This is the type of thinking, which cause failure. People like these who base their relationships on what can you do for me feel that as long as they are getting something, their relationship is good. Okay be that as it may - everybody is entitled to their own beliefs. But what happens when the person involved with this type of individual cannot or can no longer provide the service of satisfying the financial obligations of the other? Simple, the truth will come out and each party in the relationship will realize that the relationship was based on finance instead of romance and the relationship will fail. Now I am in no way attempting to make this a religious lesson but if a person were to notice that when there is religious direction, followed by family and the eradication of anything else which does not add to the happiness or longevity of the two, aren't people rather couples more often better off? I am not saying that anyone reading this should automatically go out and join any religious faction. I mean it's good if you do especially if it's not one of those hypocritical places where this member is sleeping with that member or the pastor is doing something that he doesn't want anybody in the church to know about but I'm saying that if the structure and positive reinforcement which is prevalent in many churches and religious institutions today were applied to relationships, they would be happier and consequently not ending at such breakneck speeds.

I have to talk about women for a second. Now as much as I love you crazy, sexy, triflin' females, I feel I have to verbally chastise many of you for some of your actions. One of those actions is the amount of yapping you do as well as the people you women yap to. Now in every one of my relationships as well as almost all of the relationships I am and have been aware of, the women I know have had no problem talking to damn near everybody about damn near everything. This is not always the problem. Being that I am an introverted person by nature, this level of loquaciousness proved favorable quite often. The problem comes about when women get hit on and no I don't mean physically – I mean when guys and sometimes other women hit on them in search of a meaningless physical relationship but lie and tell them they want something long term. The biggest cause of this can be attributed to people divulging their level of happiness or unhappiness to others. I can tell you firsthand about how I have been bombarded with stories of how bad some women have been treated by their significant others for example – 'he's cheating on me; or 'he's beating on me' and mind you, most of the time I didn't even ask. When a person is so willing to offer his or her disappointment to another, it should be known that that is little more than a cry for help. A person may think that he or she is just venting but it's more than that. The bad part about this is the fact that many people in this world will gladly assist in answering that cry for help by offering that person some sex – and the real bad thing about this scenario is the fact that often the person who is offered the sex will be under the impression that the one offering is really looking for a relationship. Women, if there is ever a point in your life when you feel that the only recourse you have regarding your bad relationship is to talk to someone who has nothing to do with your relationship, make sure that someone is a professional or someone who has no possible interest in a sexual exploit with you and reason being is because people lie. They lie for any reason under the sun.

People especially lie when there is something to be gained. When you put out the fact that you are unhappy, all a man with half an ounce of common sense has to do is act like he cares and the drawers are his. (For the record, this occurs with men as well as women) I am sure a lot of ladies will get mad behind that but the truth usually has that power – the power to make people mad. Women you have to be smarter than that - if for no other reason than to save yourself future heartbreak. Don't put yourself in the 'damsel in distress' mode because others will pick up on that and play 'knight in shining armor' to the rescue. Now I will be the first to admit that it's often hard to tell where a person's true intentions lie because of the extremely high level of deception in this world but a person can avoid being or appearing so openly vulnerable. One of the things I hate about this world is the 'you've attained a certain status, let's make a target out of you' thing. This applies to those high profile individuals who make millions of dollars per year as well as those who just happen to be in the public eye for something they have accomplished. The first thing that happens when a person falls into one of the above categories is he or she gets more media attention that what is necessary and often desired. This is bad because when people notice you have something or when people think you have something they want, quite often they will do anything to get some or all of what you have. This is why many celebrities either hire round the clock bodyguards or keep their finances as well as activities completely hidden. In relationships, the more a relationship is exposed, the more chance a person will have for intrusion and intervention. It is a good thing to rant sometimes – you can tell that by reading my books – lol - but sometimes no matter how much a person feels like spitting out every explicit detail of how bad her husband hurt her by cheating, that person needs to restrict that rant session. This is because just like the celebrity example above, the more people know about your situation the more likely they will know how to manipulate or exploit it as well and if the situation is properly exploited, the victim will almost never know that she was a victim. This will either cause unhappiness or add to whatever unhappiness there was in the relationship to begin with.

Revenge – An eye for an eye, a tooth for a tooth. Revenge is the nice way of saying let no one get one up on you. It is what most inner city children are taught growing up; if someone hits you, hit them back. There are many types of revenge, especially when it comes to relationships. There's the attitude revenge, as in you're mad? Okay now I'm mad too. There's the independence revenge, as in you're going out? Okay then I'm going out too. There's even the reciprocating love revenge, as in you love me? Good I love you too - you hate me? Guess what? I hate you just as much. Along with the types of revenge, there are reasons for its being. The top reason for revenge in my opinion is the therapeutic and calming effect it has on a person. Getting even with someone who has wronged you can be compared to the feelings one gets from the act of sex itself - wonderful. The only problem, rather the main problem with revenge is that it has a downside. When a person harms someone and that harmed person takes revenge on the one that has harmed him, unless both parties are adult enough and forgiving enough to let it end there, a cycle will begin, which not only may continue but in many cases spiral out of control until somebody gets really hurt or dies. It's much like the cycle of child abuse where an abuser will abuse the significant other and or the family, then the children will grow up and abuse the significant other and or family and those children will grow up and so on and so on. A person has to be able to say 'I'm going to stop this pattern of abuse' just like he must be able to say 'I will stop this cycle of revenge.' But this is the hard part. Revenge feels so satisfying. It does not just feel adequately satisfying; sometimes it feels so good that people will spend moths and years planning a vengeful act. The thing about revenge is that to accomplish it well, each party must possess that 'I have to win mindset. 'Going back to the example about inner city youth, these people must do what is done to them. Now this does not mean if somebody punches you in the face that you cannot forgive them. In fact many people, even those that are not religious will tell you this is what should be done as far as searching for the best revenge. The problem is that no one likes to have anybody else get over on them or have one up on them. This is why the act of revenge will never die. Revenge is the act of doing something to someone who has done something to you. So in short, a wronged person can do anything - from something just to teach another a lesson to something that will prevent the person from ever doing whatever was done to anybody else. The legal system usually mandates how revenge should be handled, for instance somebody tries to kill you, you can kill them but note this must be done while they are in the middle of trying to kill you. You can't wait three or four days, then apply for a handgun permit, wait for the background check to clear, as well as the required wait time for the license and other related necessities, then get the gun and go and shoot this person. That sounds like the ideal method of revenge to many people but it's not the right method. I think it has something to do with that premeditated thing. It's funny though... cause usually when one person is trying to kill another, that person is most often trying to get away. Some religious law dictates that for a person to get even with another, he or she should let it be handled by the higher power in which a person believes. But not everybody follows religious law. Some people say that they will be judge, jury and executioner - and this is because many times law enforcement is a joke, unless of course they see the infraction occurring. Sometimes revenge is mandated by the thoughts and actions of society at large. Sometimes a person will want to forgive another for a wrong committed against them but someone else will say 'they hurt someone in your family, you have to hurt somebody in theirs!' and to not be ostracized by this nosey person and his ignorant circle of influence, this person will go and hurt someone to avenge the person in his family who was hurt as well as satisfy the expectations of society. Regular revenge and infidelity revenge are closely related because they both entail getting somebody back for something that was done to them but the real interesting thing about infidelity revenge is that usually only infidelity itself or an act equal to the pain of infidelity (which is often murder) will suffice. Regular revenge is doing something. Infidelity revenge is doing something directly related to infidelity - like cutting off a penis or gluing one's penis to one's leg with a strong adhesive. Revenge is sometimes described as cold. It is sometimes described as sweet. Its definition is one of the most emotionally charged meanings in the English language. Revenge has always been slated as one of the leading causes of wars, street fights, murders and infidelity. When it comes to cheating, very few people in this world can allow themselves to be hurt without desiring vengeance and not just any run of the mill, garden variety type of vengeance but vengeance, which is equal to or greater than the level of hurt, which was bestowed upon them. The hurt which comes from infidelity is one of the few things in this world that can usually only be satisfied by forgiveness or the act itself. With few things other than age related, mental deterioration, what causes a person to desire and seek revenge cannot easily be forgotten. Ex. If a couple is involved in a relationship and the male gets caught in the act of cheating, his significant other can burn all his clothes, evict him from her place of residence and even defame his character to the entire world via the web, public access television or by posting fliers with his picture and the word cheater scrawled underneath on every tree, light post or building she can find. However, going through the trouble of all the aforementioned tactics will rarely provide the woman with the same level of satisfaction as that of indulging in an affair, equal to that of her mate and letting him find out about it. Ex. 2 - If a person steals your brand new bike and you, as a child, get severely punished for it, having the person who stole it apologize years later will not eradicate the memory of the bike nor will it eradicate the memory of the punishment. What will help somewhat is taking something that belongs to and means a lot to that person – to show them how it feels. What will help more is beating that person's ass so that they can experience a snippet of the level of pain that you yourself had to experience as a child. (I'm just joking - I would never advocate violence as a way of settling problems!) But the thought does make a person feel good sometimes. This is the main idea behind the revenge cycle -

I feel good. Somebody hurts me, now they feel good about hurting me. I feel bad now because they hurt me
So I get revenge on them so I can again feel good.

People can look at someone who has been hurt, victimized, traumatized – whatever and say they sympathize but there are certain types of hurt, which must be felt to be understood. People must remember that everything they do in life has consequences. Some consequences are good, some are bad. Some consequences are immediate and some don't take effect until the afterlife but every action causes some kind of reaction. When a person is cheated on, several factors come into play. It is not just the fact that a bad act occurred, it is more the fact that a betrayal of trust, a breaking of the heart and even the smashing of the bond of fidelity has allowed itself to happen. The factors coming into play make it harder for a person to just be able to say 'okay I forgive you' or 'it's alright, I'll get over it.' These factors make a person hurt and not only do they make someone hurt they make that person want to hurt the one who hurt them....bad. This is what I believe to be the top reason why infidelity scares people the way it does. You see when a person is hurt, no one, especially that hurt person knows in what manner he or she will respond - if that person responds at all. Historically, the level of hurt someone bestows upon another would usually determine if and how much revenge there would be dished out to the original party. Let's say someone took a key and scratched your nice, shiny new car. The appropriate level of vengeance would be to either scratch their car or if you are like me and not a fan of the police, break a window or two. With infidelity however, it's different. People die over infidelity. And that's a big stretch from scratching somebody's car. What's the difference? With infidelity, feelings are involved. Now of course there are feelings involved when a car gets damaged, especially if it's a new car. But how many people will kill over a scratch on that new car as opposed to a husband or wife's infidelity? A scratch can easily be repaired. A stolen car can even be forgiven - but when a wife screws around on a husband with his best friend or when a husband fools around on his wife - that type of pain can last forever. There are several types of revenge I have seen used on the significant other when it comes to infidelity. Some of the more popular ones include damaging someone's vehicle, having an affair and letting the significant other know about it, having an affair and letting the significant other find out about it on his or her own or contracting an std and continuing to sleep with the significant other. I am sure there are many of you reading this who will say things like that's nasty - no one in his or her right mind would go so far as to hurt themselves just to hurt someone who has hurt them. If you are one of those people who believe that, let me be the first to tell you that when people are driven by revenge, they are never in their right minds! A man who has been or who feels he has been cheated on by his significant other will go and sleep with someone just to get even and if that man is unable to immediately sleep with the woman of his choice, he may hire a prostitute who may just happen to have one or maybe many sexually transmitted diseases. Now initially, it may not be his intent to infect his wife or girlfriend with whatever he has acquired from the hooker but what if he does not know he has contracted something? He could be sleeping with the significant other for years and years until one day during happier times the infection presents itself outwardly and he thinks that the significant other being unfaithful has given it to him. On the other hand, what if he does know and doesn't care? As I mentioned earlier, when driven by revenge, people are not in their right minds. Revenge will always be a factor in why people cheat but what is an even bigger factor is the mistaken thought of what might be infidelity. A lot of people think they know more than they actually do. These people will often think that infidelity is occurring and will respond with infidelity of their own even if there is no proof to substantiate their feelings. Suspicions, combined with an impulsive nature, as well as no communication, will create problems. People have to be open with one another. This means that if a person feels that something is going on regarding infidelity, then that person should be able to communicate those feelings to the suspected significant other and the significant other should be open and willing enough to address them.

Excitement – The one thing I find, which is almost universally feared among committed couples, is boredom. Boredom is a feeling of irritability, which comes from either being continually exposed to something uninteresting or because of having nothing to do. It's said that a person who is bored is often a boring person himself but in a relationship a bored person who has nothing to do, may classify their partner as the uninteresting one and blame them for their own situation. People fear boredom so much because by definition, it describes the feeling you get when you have nothing to do, yet the one thing it does do is give a person the initiative to go looking for something to excite them. All too often that something turns into someone. As I mentioned earlier, a person can learn something from everybody in this world and that's because everybody in this world knows at least one thing another person doesn't. Boredom in relationships sometimes happens when you get to know a person too well. That's also the time they become predictable and when 'nothing they say or do interests you.' Then, the first person outside that relationship who comes with something, which the other has not heard or experienced, will seem more interesting and possibly more attractive than their bored counterpart at home. I've seen this happen too many times – When a couple gets together, changes take place on the side of each partner. This can be looked at as both, a good and bad thing because out of all of the couples I know, not one of them likes everything about the one they're involved with. A certain level of adjustment must always be made in relationships for each other's benefit. Change, in that respect is good because the ultimate goal resulting from that change is peace of mind in their relationship but when people 'change' too much, they lose sight of what they had, just to please the other person and as a result are miserable because of it. Fun things at the beginning of relationships are often dangerous but a person will get involved with a person who does these fun and or dangerous things, then after the feelings start to form and solidify, the sensible person will put forth whatever effort necessary to stop those fun and or dangerous things from occurring. Wearing tight, revealing clothing for example, comes to an abrupt stop after involvement in some relationships or if not an abrupt stop, then comes at least the attempt to stop it. The thing that causes problems is that when these people who like wearing the tight, revealing clothing meet up with those who don't mind that type of gear and a connection or attraction forms because of that fact. Then it becomes a situation of 'my boyfriend is too old school – he's not hip like you.' And once that connection or attraction forms, the door is left wide open for possibly infidelity. People who perform tricks on motorcycles or drive excessively fast in their cars or even spend money recklessly; change when they get involved in certain relationships and this is basically to keep their partner or to keep their partner happy. When a person who has seen this type of behavior from their partner and the behavior changes for whatever reason, the other person will be attracted to whatever person indulges in the former fun activity. Boredom causes people to change and many times this is good but as with everything else in life, there must be a balance. If a person changes or is forced to change an excessive amount, they will not be happy with themselves as well as not be happy with the person who caused them to change. If the change a person in a relationship makes is not significant enough, the other party may not find continued interest. Many people believe boredom is completely and utterly responsible for things like the introduction of toys in the bedroom and swapping partners for sex. And this is often because the traditional lovemaking methods, which are afforded to most committed couples, die out all too soon. Excitement is renewed with people who wish to remain monogamous when they usher in marital assistance tools. The couples that do not entirely care about monogamy enjoy their own brand of excitement as well. This is accomplished by using the energy, which can only come from another person or couple. A lot of people still don't realize that the mind is heavily connected to the sexual organs. Just like many women are always griping and moaning about their emotional needs and such, after a period of time, men need more than just visual stimulation to keep the fires burning. It is more than just 'hard' for someone to be sexually attracted to a person he or she is not or no longer interested in. The big belief in relationships today is that women need to be aroused to a certain point before they can fully enjoy the sex act but men are supposed to see a naked woman and instantly be ready. For some men, that type of visual stimulation may work well when the relationship is new but after seeing the same person get naked for years upon years, having them strip and bend over will not provide the same level of arousal or satisfaction. Women are famous for stopping sex whenever it becomes stale or monotonous. Men are famous for using excuses like 'she doesn't give me none anymore' or 'she doesn't do what she used to at the beginning of our relationship anymore' but men will also stop the flow of intimacy if the same stale or monotonous feelings apply. People for some reason or another believe that the act of sex is one of the most powerful things in this world and I must agree, the effects are quite powerful but the powers of the sex act are overshadowed by the physical longevity. When you get right down to it, a committed relationship usually involves a man and a woman. The longer that man and that woman are together, the stronger the commitment is believed to be. Each person can do but so much to keep the relationship interesting after so many years of doing the same thing. When people say they have cheated because their own sexual relationship was boring beyond repair, I can't personally condone the action but I can see my way to understanding. How miserable would an existence be if people were forced to live with only what they presently have and never be able to experience something better or at least different? Fun and immediate gratification will always be heavily desired in this world but things like stability, safety and long-term satisfaction will always win out when it comes to necessity.

If there is something to be gained by acting a certain way, whether it is potentially detrimental or not, people will do it. That's why it is very possible to see undercover racists working as members of law enforcement or pedophiles working in schools. I cannot say it enough, deception is so powerful that people may change their lives based on it. I also believe that people have an innate need to be happy and or comfortable. If certain people are happy and or comfortable with two partners instead of one, as long as neither partner complains, they will do whatever it takes to make that happiness continue. To again touch on the 'cloud of complacency' on which many people reside, I've noticed that there are many out here who are scared of knowing the truth about what may actually be happening in their relationships. In fact they are more than just scared; they are petrified. These people fear truth because truth is definitive. Truth is painful. Truth is now. Truth blasts away the fantasy world millions of us live in everyday. Truth dictates many things. The cold harsh reality of truth dictates that one or more people reading these words may die before they finish. Few people want to accept that. The majority of people in this world want to believe that death is never close. They want to believe that death is far away, residing in the same apartment complex as sickness or old age. These people are in denial. Death can happen right now. Truth also dictates that no relationship is immune from infidelity. Few people want to accept that also. Many folks refuse to believe that infidelity is always a possibility due to the fact that they have let high levels of good times and deception cloud their better sense of judgment. Infidelity, like death, needs no appointment, calling card or prior arrangement. Infidelity can happen to you or anyone you know and at any time. There are many illusion causing techniques, perpetrated by the media, which allow infidelity to continue. Many people are lulled into thinking that an affair must be extravagant. They think that for an affair to take place, there must be a limousine carrying the perfectly proportioned male to the five star hotel of the conveniently unsatisfied spouse, where after a few glasses of champagne and a bubble bath, the two will retire to the bedroom for hours upon hours of passionate and fulfilling lovemaking before one of the two has to rush home to the unknowing significant other. These people do not want to accept the fact that an affair is also a male giving a drug addicted female twenty dollars for her to pull down her pants and bend over in some staircase while he releases some pent up frustration. This is truth. This is reality. This is what people in relationships fear. As long as the relationship situation is comfortable, meaning as long as there are no arguments or things, which would likely cause arguments, the belief is that the relationship is good and or happy. These people are so closed minded or confused that they desire to decipher if their husband or wife is cheating but they run like the wind when offered the opportunity to learn how to commit an indiscretion. Forgive me for asking an obvious question here but aren't they both pretty much the same? If someone writes a book with the title 'How To Catch Someone Cheating' and another person writes a book entitled 'The Correct Way To Fool Around' what difference is there other than people's perceptions? People always say they wouldn't be interested in learning about cheating but when I ask why, I hear everything from 'knowledge leads to activity' to 'I don't want to let the spirit of infidelity enter into the relationship.' Those answers are somewhat acceptable but not completely logical. What is not acceptable or understandable is how these same people will turn right around and say they will read something called 'How To Catch Someone Cheating.' If there is a book with that actual title in circulation, please understand I'm not trying to hate, I just need somebody to explain the logic. Certain law enforcement agencies, when trying to track down a suspected criminal will often use the 'if I were a criminal, what would I do' method to catch said suspected criminal. These law enforcement agencies use this tactic to get into the mind of a criminal and if this does not work, they do the next best thing, confer with an actual criminal who is guilty of the same type of activity. Serial killers for example are often recruited or studied to gain insight on other more elusive serial killers. Past methods of incarcerated thieves are often used to help catch current ones. On the same token, I believe the best way to catch a cheater is to confer with cheaters and the people who have been in relationships with them and find out what motivates them as well as their methods. The difference with the two books stated above is that the first one (How To Catch Someone Cheating) gives the impression that whoever reads it probably already suspects someone of infidelity and wants to find out how to catch them. The second (The Correct Way To Fool Around 2) gives the impression that someone just wants to learn how to cheat. Now both titles cover or should cover the same topic, learning about infidelity, just one (How To Catch...) would probably put the information in fifth grade, simpleton language whereas the other (The Correct Way...) requires people use their brains to find out it's the same thing. If someone tells you that these are some of the tricks people use to covertly commit a transgression, wouldn't you want to know if those tricks were being used on you? The problem with too many people is that they feel their brains have daily limits on use. They feel that if they were to exceed these limits, their brains would probably shut down from exertion. If more people used their brains to look at the bigger picture, rather than only what's directly in front of their already disillusioned faces, there probably, no there definitely wouldn't be as high a level of infidelity as what presently exists.

People in relationships are always wondering what would make a person cheat. These people continue to wonder if they did something wrong to cause their significant other to cheat if that is or has been the case. What a lot of these people do not realize is that they could be 'perfect' as far as what many people outside of that relationship are looking for. What these people do not also realize is that many of the people they get involved with may have deep routed emotional issues. These are issues, which could have stemmed from their childhood, issues, which could have stemmed from past relationships or issues, which were simply never resolved. As I always try and explain, there are so many reasons, which cause infidelity that I do not believe one person could list them all just as I do not believe one person could list all the methods. One reason I know to be true is the excitability factor. There's one certainty that can be said about life, aside from the death and taxes thing and that's the realization that if you continue to do the same thing day after day be it employment or enjoyment, eventually you will find yourself in a rut. I have asked people on numerous occasions, if they had a choice of any job in this world to perform eight hours a day, five days a week, fifty one weeks out of the year- with one week off for vacation - what would it be? Almost all of them said either I don't know or travel to different places. The operative word there being different. As surprising as it was, nobody mentioned being a porn star or the sex industry. Yet when I asked these same people what their dream job would be where they could make their own hours, most of them responded with that field - well most of the men any way. The point I am trying to make here is that people, men and women, will do things they like, even things they love only for a certain amount of time until they either get completely bored or into a pattern of learned helplessness, where their mind tells them that they cannot do any better or any different. A prime example is some of the people who live in certain buildings in certain neighborhoods. Anybody who has lived in, visited, driven by or seen pictures of some of the front of these buildings on a summer day can tell you they are usually swamped with residents. I don't find too much wrong with that - I mean if that's your place of residence, you should be able to stand or sit in front of it as you damn well please but some of these people act like it is their job to be the eyes, noses and ears of the community, meaning seeing and hearing what goes on in the area and then reporting it to whoever will listen. Again, if that's where you live and that's what you choose to do by all means be my guest - but what I have observed is that many of these people who magnetize themselves to the front of their buildings do so because they have nothing else to do. They are longing for excitement, something, which will snatch them from the everyday, propelling them into a state of temporary bliss, then returning them back to their hum drum lives, ever so satisfied, kinda the way cheating does. Another example of this is dealing with a virgin. Virgin sex is one of the most special, coveted and desired things in this world and why, because it's new. It's exciting - it's the 'I don't know what I'm gonna get. I don't know if I'm gonna like it or hate it. I just know I am eagerly and impulsively waiting for it.' People who are lucky enough to have a relationship with someone who has never had intercourse before are seen as gods. They are exalted and why, because they have achieved something that many others wish for. They have experienced new. Sex is one of those things which is new only once - unless of course it is with somebody else. The euphoric high which comes from the first time sex is had begins to wane each and every time thereafter. People try things to enhance the sexual experience like toys and gadgets and role play and such - some even going so far as to invite someone else into their bedroom for a threesome. This is done simply because as good as sex is, no matter how much a person does it, it will never be new after its not. People are always asking how can the one they are involved in a relationship with ever desire somebody else or how can this person ever not find interest in the significant other or even why do intimacy levels fluctuate? There is I believe one simple reason; because we're human. We do what we are taught. As children, how many of us have only one toy to play with? How many of us have only one outfit or one type of meal everyday? The answer is none. And this is simply because we need variety. We cannot exist on one type of anything without desiring something else - especially if that is how we have been conditioned. This does not mean that we have to act on our desires; it just means that they will always be there. New is what keeps a relationship interesting. When people dine, they have the option of going to the same restaurant, which they always frequent or they can try somewhere new each time. Going to the same one makes people feel comfortable. Going to a new one provides a person with wonder. The atmosphere will be different, the food will be different and even the people in the establishment will differ as well. This is one of the things people look for when they cheat. It is not the only thing because there are many cheaters who have long time affairs with just one person and the reasons why the affair continues extend way beyond new sex. Using this type of logic, the 'it meant nothing' excuse may not be so hard to believe when it's a one time thing. I am not saying its right or acceptable, I'm just saying that it is more believable than a person in a relationship having an affair for a few months or a few years and trying to use that same excuse.

Lack of Intimacy – There is a belief in this world that love never dies. This belief has been known to span years, miles and negative mindsets. The belief of many people is that true love lasts until the end of time – not until the end of marriage but until both parties are no longer a part of this world and beyond. Yes, there are those who believe that if a couple were involved in true love, they would still be together in the afterlife. I for one have no clue to whether this is true or not but I will say it seems to be the epitome of wishful thinking. Love is believed to always be at its highest level of intensity whenever it is shared. Unfortunately that belief rarely extends into the world of physical intimacy. The levels of intimacy in relationships have been known to fluctuate like the Dow Jones Industrial Average and this depends, not upon how in love a couple is but how happy said couple is at any given moment. One of the sad but true facts in this world is that many people in relationships will get to a point where they no longer find sexual interest in one another. Another sad but true fact is that many of these people will base their entire relationship or a good portion of it on sex. There are certain things which can make intimacy wane, for instance people will get bored of one another after a certain amount of time or they regret committing themselves at such a young age or they have kids – a definite intimacy stealer. The fact that they have nothing else to 'fall back on' relationship wise can lead the couple to seek out other parties for physical intimacy. This can affect one person or both parties. A person's type of employment or time committed to employment can have damaging effects on how high intimacy levels rise. Now while it's well known that many relationships start out based on intimacy, what's not always known is that the levels will not continue on the same wavelength throughout the union. Aside from career and family, there are many things, which may become severe stumbling blocks when it comes to intimacy. Infidelity, for example will always cause a break in the chain of intimacy. Two reasons; one, when a person cheats, unless they have an endless supply of Viagra or endurance, it will be very difficult to keep up the level of lovemaking the committed couple may have shared before the transgression and two, if a person is caught cheating, there will be a significant lapse in intimacies because of 'the waiting game.' This is where the guilty party will have to apologize to, cater to, and make up to the innocent party for the length of the lapse. The bad part is the innocent party will almost always dictate the length of the lapse of intimacy.

Some people often use intimacy or should I say the lack of as punishment when their partner does or says something, which they do not like. Now when it comes to disrespect, as in verbal or physical abuse, I can see the withholding of intimacies as a just punishment but very few other reasons, I believe warrant that type of treatment. What all too often happens in relationships is that one person will ask the other for something, as in helping out with housework or maybe they'll ask for what could be considered a lot of money, to which their partner will answer 'no.' The requesting but denied party will then take that 'no' as a personal attack and respond with not giving up the goodies. These 'goodie withholders' belong to a very popular club. The 'I'm disillusioned because I believe my significant other would never, ever cheat on me' club. Some couples have very different views on sex when they get together, which is not exactly the problem. The problem is that many of these couples don't always they don't talk about them before they become committed. There are some people who believe that sex was meant to be more procreation than recreation. There are others who believe just the opposite. Everybody in a relationship is entitled to their opinion or belief but having two different beliefs on something as important as sex is to some people can have detrimental effects to that relationship. Aside from people being disillusioned into believing their partners are incapable of cheating on them, I believe people find it so easy to withhold sex from their partner because they don't hold sex in as high regard as their mates. Some people feel sex is a reward for a job well done, as in washing the other's car or for not expressing one's dislike for their in laws while they visit. Other people feel sex is an unwritten contractual obligation - as in 'if we have sex, you gotta clean up the house.' As I mentioned before, everybody is more than entitled to their beliefs on the amounts of intimacy they feel are appropriate, the only problem is these people don't discuss their beliefs with the person with whom they will be or are presently sharing intimacies with. There will <u>always</u> be disagreements when it comes to sex. There will be disagreements on favorite positions, time spent in favorite positions and where sex in those favorite positions is being had. The biggest disagreement will be how often and this disagreement <u>will</u> come about because people are different. Nobody always desires sexual intercourse the same amount or at the same time as their significant other. Many people in relationships do have sex whenever their partner requests but this is generally to appease that partner and not themselves. The <u>only</u> way a couple will not have issues with the amount of physical intimacy they share is if they put it in writing – a sex prenuptial if you will. (Example shown in my second book, Relationships Pacification for crazy people - page 78.) A little piece of paper put in place before the commitment is consummated will generally alleviate any problems dealing with frequency. It will not however help the mechanical and structured feeling of intercourse, which is sure to come.

.

Chapter Two
How Not To Get Caught...

Most of us were taught in school, several nursery rhymes, adages and sayings, which we still use today in adult life. Those sayings were intended to teach us lessons, which were supposed to help carry us successfully through adulthood. Many of the sayings ranged from time saving, like killing two birds with one stone to informative, like a bird in the hand is better than two in the bush - to harsh, like a hard head makes a soft behind. Amidst the multitude of sayings were two, which stuck out in my mind for some reason or another and those were: never judge a book by its cover and sticks and stones can break my bones but words can never hurt me. I remember as maybe most young people hearing these for the first time and not completely understanding or maybe understanding and not heeding. When I reached maturity however, I garnered a greater grasp of these two sayings and they have both left me with one united expression, rather feeling of my own. That feeling was 'what a crock of shit!' Let's examine: Never judging a book by its cover can apply to a person's race, as well as their abilities, as well as an actual book, among other things. My interpretation of this saying is don't assume that all; which is displayed is all, which is contained because someone or something can show you a side which is totally contradictory to its other side. 'Sticks and stones can break my bones but words can never hurt me' is in my opinion an even bigger crock of shit. The reason I consider these sayings so untrue and derogatory is that aside from the fact that almost no one over the age of ten takes them to heart; they are totally contradictory to their proposed meaning in many instances. For example - and I'm using the above sticks and stones adage, if people are so supposedly impervious to words, why is it that a little six letter word, (more commonly known as the 'N' word) when directed at the black community by someone not of the black community can incite violence or at least feelings of hatred, whether those feelings be at one's self or toward the person throwing the slur? Is it because that word actually does have power and not just a little inkling of power but power to where it can almost demoralize an entire society by it's very mention? Or is it because people of African American descent are too selectively sensitive? I doubt seriously if it is an issue of sensitivity because if that were actually the case, the word would be equally damaging – no matter who used it. Unfortunately life is not like that. Maybe people don't completely realize how important some issues are to others or maybe people are just fucking retarded. Think about it, people say 'what's up my nigga?' all the time and almost nobody raises an eyebrow – yet many of these people who use and accept the term understand that it originally had a negative connotation associated with it. The term 'piece of shit' has historically been associated with nothing positive either yet you don't hear anybody saying 'what's up you piece of shit?' Funny both terms are degrading and one is often used to classify an entire race of people but I doubt seriously if anybody would allow the piece of shit term to be used in daily conversation, whether it was by a white person directed at someone black or by a black person to someone of his own race. (Then again I could just be rambling.) I think many people don't say anything because they fear the consequences of showing those who use that term just how high their level of ignorance actually is or it could be the fact that people get complacent and accept the fact that the situation will more than likely never change. Here's another question about 'power having' words; Why is it that one word can instantly attract the attention of law enforcement and government officials, that word being terrorism or more specifically Al Queda? Is it because the last example, even though they are a particular group, was believed to have been behind one of the most deadly attacks in recent memory? Or is it that we have become scared to the point of if any one shows any type of interest in that last example other than unfavorable, that person must be ostracized and/or possibly put on a government watch list? Now even though these may be extreme examples, the point, which is jockeying for recognition is that certain words, whether they're groups or not, are more damaging and contain more power than many people give them credit for. One of those especially damaging words is 'predictability.' The worst thing in a relationship for some people is the stigma of being predictable or having their partners being able to say 'I cheated on my mate so many times because I know him or her so well.' Predictability is one of the main weapons a person uses when involving themselves in an affair because it can be used both ways - to a person's advantage as well as to their detriment. To be successful at cheating, you must remember certain things. One of the most advisable methods in which to avoid detection is by doing exactly what people normally expect from you. Reason being, people will watch your actions and use them to label what type of person they believe you are. If you are a person who goes to church every week, people who do not personally know you but see you going to church will generally assume one of three things; 1) that you are a good person. 2) If not a good person, then someone who is attempting to get their life on the proper track. 3) You are a low life who is attempting to meet a 'good' man or woman in the church. If for instance you are a 'family man' who goes to work every day from nine to five and returns home at exactly 6:15pm, Monday to Friday, with a weekly bouquet of flowers for the wife, people who do not personally know you will most likely assume that you are a faithful and family oriented person. The above may be true examples of people's lives. Then again, they may be part of the mass deception, which many people are a part of today. People must remember that everything in this world can be looked at two ways, the truth and a front to dissuade someone from the truth. This is what's so wonderful and at the same time confusing about infidelity. You never know when someone is telling the truth unless you consistently follow him or her or unless you are an expert on brain fingerprinting. Using the above examples, a person can leave for church every week but never get there. That person may be using 'going to church' as a technique to get out of the house, away from a nagging, atheist wife. The atheist wife may unwittingly be helping the husband commit his transgressions because of her beliefs. Due to the fact that atheists do not believe in God, they will have little reason to be attending Sunday service other than to heckle the worshippers. This example is purely hypothetical because nine times out of ten, a devout churchgoer would rarely be involved with someone on the opposite end of the spectrum. There is always the possibility however that both individuals were married as atheists and one is attempting to find or renew lost faith, then again, as stated above, the 'churchgoer' could just be using that reason and opportunity to escape. The person who goes to 'work' Monday to Friday, may in actuality only work Monday to Wednesday and use the last two days of the week to spend time with someone else – thereby giving credibility to the 'he's only bringing flowers home because he's cheating or because he messed up' thing. People's daily patterns are what either makes or breaks them when it comes to infidelity. If you give a person little or no reason to believe you are capable of doing wrong, chances are they will believe just that. Everybody in this world knows or should know that infallibility is something that no one can attain. People also know or should know that everyone makes mistakes and everyone is capable of failure. What these people do however is let a person's actions dictate the level of assurance when it comes to how good or bad certain other people are. A person or many people in fact, who only sees somebody doing good may be lulled into believing that that is all that person is capable of doing. Little Mrs. Johnson, whom everybody believes is the best babysitter in the neighborhood, will be just that until she is caught by a nanny cam beating the hell out of one of the neighborhood kids in her care. People by nature, unless given reason to think otherwise, generally look for the good in others. (Innocent until proven guilty) If you get caught in sticky situations or tell of past situations, in which you have done wrong and with no retribution, people will more than likely be prompted to believe that you will continue that pattern. For instance, what if a man were to say 'I cheated on every woman I ever dealt with.' Would this man be the optimal trust figure? Of course not. Even if this man goes cold turkey and decides never to cheat again, the fact that he has publicly spoken those words will make most who have heard them believe that he is incapable of change. On the same note, if a person gets caught publicly in a sex scandal whether by his or her own admission or by a well crafted plan, people will label that person based on that indiscretion and will more often than not use the methods of past society and judge the guilty party's abilities at rehabilitation based on others who have failed as well. Since most who get involved in infidelity based relationships usually have no chance at getting back together, many people will automatically say the same holds true for anybody else who does the same crime.

What too many people in natural (cheating) relationships do is 'change' when they commit certain transgressions. The change can be in attitude or in activities. Whatever the case, change causes people to notice. Falling into the realm of predictability can be one of the best things in the world to do if you plan to cheat. Reason being; if you are so set in your ways that your partner can plan his or her activities by your schedule, chances are they know your actions better than you do. Most people do things because they're second nature. These things require little thought. They are instinctive. Putting on your clothes, brushing your hair or knowing where you normally put your keys when you enter your home all fall into the second nature category. If you are trying to cover up your tracks after committing an indiscretion, chances are you will have to think about what you normally do in order to try and perfect things so as not to arouse suspicion. The problem with this is that when you try to re enact what comes naturally; you need to have an almost impeccable memory. Most of the people in this world don't. Many people, although they may think they thrive under pressure, don't realize that when they rush or are placed in stressful situations, things are often forgotten. Putting on one's clothes in a hurried state can lead to an inside out t-shirt or worse, inside out panties. Now while the person committing the indiscretion may not think twice about the tag on the panty being on the left as opposed to the right or vice versa, the husband or significant other of this person may. And what possible reason can someone who has been cheating give to a very observant significant other when she gets home with her panties on backwards? What people need to do in relationships, infidelity based or otherwise is take time. There needs to be time to create infidelity, time to clean up after infidelity and most importantly time to hide all traces of the fact that infidelity has ever occurred. In a regular relationship, people need to take time to get to know each other, they need to take time to get to know what makes each other different and what ticks each other off. In a regular relationship, people also need to know where the relationship is going and where each party wants it to go. The time it takes to accomplish all of these things is what helps a relationship's existence. When people don't take time in relationships, the relationships always fail or if they don't fail, then they are not happy. In infidelity based relationships if no time is taken, the relationship will fail as well and the best method of proof is that of everybody who has been caught cheating. If a person were to actually take a poll on the reasons why the cheating relationship failed, the number one reason would be because the party or parties involved didn't take time to cover their tracks or didn't take time to prepare or didn't take time to do something. The bottom line here is that time is imperative, necessary and crucial. Brushing one's hair may not seem like anything to raise an eyebrow over but the fact that the act seems so insignificant, may make people forget that a woman's hair often remains entangled in the brush after doing so. If a married man's wife has blonde hair and there's red or black hair in the brush, that will definitely be cause for concern. If keys, which are normally placed on a key ring or a specific table, are for some reason or other placed let's say, on the living room table or in the bedroom, then questions may be raised as to why. Unless a person can come up with an airtight alibi or unquestionable answer as to why the keys were someplace other than where they normally rest, there will be questions. Questions lead to doubt and doubt is first cousin to suspicion. Something as small as being late without an explanation or without a plausible one at least can raise a certain level of doubt in many relationships. You, the cheater must never allow yourself to fall into or be forced into an unpredictable situation. What you can and should do is have everyone around you believe that you are too simple or too set in your ways to ever deviate from the pattern, which people believe is your life. You must take note of what you do as well as take note of how long it takes for you to do it. Before you commit your indiscretion, you should already have a timetable of your daily activities, so that whenever you do commit whatever indiscretion you are planning, not one hair of suspicion will be raised. In addition to this you should also have a mental timetable of how long it takes for the significant other to accomplish his or her daily tasks as well. Always leave room for error too. This means implement a 'what if' strategy just in case your mental timetable doesn't exactly work out. This goes back to the deception described in chapter one. For example, if a married person has just finished cheating with someone in his or her home and the person that he or she has cheated with is not yet ready to leave but the significant other of that married person is on the way home, a mental timetable of how long it will take to get that person out of the house and clean up just won't do. This is what's called having ink spilled onto your blueprints. A person, especially if they don't know you are involved with another but suspect you are can hang around in your home just to see who shows up. People are funny like that. And the main reason they do this is because (and I know many of you won't believe me but...) feelings are always involved when people have sex. This is why I say always be upfront with whoever you are cheating with. It will eliminate problems and misunderstandings later. In a situation such as this where a natural partner does not want to immediately leave after sex for whatever reason, you have to resort to desperate measures. Treat him or her like an unwelcome guest because in actuality, after sex, that's all they really are. Call the police and tell them that someone is on your property either making threats, attempting to blackmail you into sex or because of sex or whatever. Basically state that they have overstayed their welcome and you want them out. The bottom line is to get them out of the house. You can lie to your significant other later about why this person was there as well as the police activity if it should ever come to that but since you've probably read my first book you should already know to have bases covered in advance. You should also know that this will pretty much end any and all chance of you sleeping with this person again unless they are just that damned desperate and if they are that damned desperate, you probably shouldn't be sleeping with them in the first place. If you don't really crave police involvement and you happen to have a stable of accomplices aka neighbors who will lie for you, you can quickly call one or more who you would already have on standby to come over and even the playing field. These neighbors could do any of a number of things, from pretending to be the husband or wife and flying into a jealous rage when they see the natural partner to just being someone who happens to drop by and be automatically and relentlessly interested in the natural partner. (This person's job will be to show so much interest in the natural partner that he or she becomes totally uncomfortable and leaves, thereby providing a safe and clear path for the actual husband or wife to come home without aggravation or suspicion.) A person must live deception, not just while they are being natural with one individual but before during and after that relationship, so that people who do not know the real you will believe you are whoever it is you pretend to be. If you are a saint in New York, then be a sinner in New Jersey. If you are an axe murderer in Canada, then be 'soccer mom' in your hometown of Buffalo. There's a saying, 'don't shit where you sleep.' This saying basically reinforces the two prior examples. People usually believe all of what they see and only a certain percentage of what they hear. If people in your particular neighborhood see you doing something bad, what's to stop them from believing it? If however, you do something derogatory where nobody knows you and someone who does know you, hears about it, then they have but two choices; believe what they already know about you, which if you are a proficient liar, will be only positive things or believe the hearsay. Most people will dispute hearsay as opposed to first hand accounts. Remember, if you are never observed doing anything wrong, the belief will be that you are incapable of doing so. When a person cheats, they will have to become a master planner - an expert at budgeting, if you will. That person will have to fit someone else into their schedule, budget enough time to adequately satisfy that person, as well as the other person in their relationship and all without raising one hair of suspicion in their circle of friends & family and within the collection of nosey neighbors sure to be lurking about. Infidelity is not easy.

One of the truest statements in life is 'unexpected things are always going to happen.' Preparation is essential and sometimes crucial for success in life. Occurrences like death, accidents and police involvement don't always require an invitation, especially if you live in New York. (Lol) Some of these things are unfortunately unavoidable and even though you may not be able to escape them, you can more than adequately plan for them. A person must prepare for work, relationships and times of adversity – for instance death. In death, a person must prepare for their own, so as not to leave an unbearable financial burden on loved ones. With regard to death, which is the most popularly unavoidable situation in the world, a good idea would be to obtain a decent amount of insurance now that you are living. It also wouldn't be such a bad idea to get one's religious house in order, depending upon one's view of the afterlife. With regard to accidents, if in a car, a cell phone, first aid kit or fire extinguisher would be helpful and when it comes to police involvement, a good attorney on hand, before the need arises is never a bad idea. When it comes to things classified as 'not so serious' a person should be just as prepared. For instance, when a man approaches a woman he is interested in, if he is not adequately prepared, chances are the woman will pick up on his awkwardness and view that as a lack of confidence. I've noticed through several attempts and conversations, (yes personal) that a lot of women don't like that. If a person is not adequately prepared for an altercation, chances are that person will get beat up, badly. If a person is not adequately prepared on the telephone, chances are they will destroy any natural relationship they are involved in. For instance, many people will call their natural partners from a phone, which allows caller ID and act surprised when someone else answers the phone. Both of these are dead giveaways. First, If a name shows up on the caller ID, your partner may write that name & number down somewhere for future reference – especially if they already suspect you. Second, if your partner does happen to see a name and number on the caller ID and they write it down and you lie about it later, that will create doubt. As habitually forgetful as some people may claim to be or actually be, doubt and what causes it in a relationship, is rarely forgotten. When a person calls the number of a specific gender, let's say female and someone of the opposite gender answers the phone, many times the caller will be caught off guard. This is a natural reflex, which happens to most people. However, that reflex, which often causes a noticeable pause, is just enough to create doubt in the mind of the person who did actually answer the phone. What people have a habit of doing when they call somebody and expect to hear one voice but in fact hear another, is apologize and assume they misdialed, often out loud. That's bad but not as bad as what these ignoramuses do next. They call right back, from the same number and then if the same person answers, these fools ask for the intended party. Where they mess up at is calling back. Making the primary call and asking for the person you intend to speak to is correct and is what should be done. However, what these people do is call, say duh, I think I got the wrong number or hang up, then call back from the same number, not more than a minute later and say something stupid like 'um, yeah, can I speak to Sabrina?' or whoever. Understand, the first call brings doubt - doubt, which is compounded by the second call. This puts the intended party in a compromising position because if they are in the vicinity of the significant other who answered the call, they will have to make up a believable story quickly to a) get the caller off the phone and b) explain to the significant other why the caller acted and/or responded the way they did.

Because of the title of my first book, The Correct Way To Fool Around, the most often question I would be asked was just that – is there a correct way to fool around and if so, what is it? I consistently found myself having to explain to people that there is no one 'correct' way to commit infidelity other than 'not getting caught.' To simply answer that question, I would have to say that The Correct Way To Fool Around is a violation of people's trust, by an array of methods and a team effort. The 'violation of trust' is a fancy way of saying betrayal. An 'array of methods' is everything in chapters two and five in this book and chapter two in my first book, The Correct Way to Fool Around. A 'team effort' is the combined efforts of you, the adulterer and a willing partner who is capable of keeping a long term secret. There are three things every person involved in, thinking about becoming involved in or who has been involved in an affair should never forget. In order of importance, they are the cell phone, purse or wallet and keys. The cell phone is most important because it is a virtual lifeline to cheaters and disorganized people. If left in the vicinity of a suspicious significant other, the significant other can go through the phone, if there's no lock code, record unfamiliar numbers of the opposite sex and use them against you for later aggravation and by this I mean calling those numbers with whom they are unfamiliar and making up some story or some question like 'hi, is Trina there' to get the person on the other end to divulge the nature of their relationship with your significant other. And when the other says who is this or how did you get this number, there will be no hesitation at all from the significant other who will emphatically say something to the effect of 'I'm her husband' or 'I'm his wife and I went through their cell phone and found your number.' People have no problem showing their jealousy at times. They may try and disguise it by saying they're 'concerned' but we all know better, they just wanna catch you cheating. There is also the worry of them answering your phone. If you were smart and informed your natural partner or partners that you were involved in a committed relationship and informed them that they (the natural partners) were only around for weekend stimulation, they would know how to speak on the phone so as not to arouse suspicion – but just as most people only use a certain percentage of computers, the same amount of people only use a certain percentage of their brains. People who do not inform the natural partners about their husbands or wives are just asking for trouble because if the cell phone of a cheater is left at the home of the person they're cheating with and the husband or wife of the cheater calls, what's to stop them from answering it? The person involved in the affair, whose home the cell phone is left at may answer the phone thinking it is their adulterous partner calling to see where he or she left it. Heaven forbid the husband or wife acquaint themselves with the natural partner over the phone. What possible defense can the cheater use? Not to mention, they are quite possibly looking at an ass whippin' from the husband or wife, as well as the other party involved in the affair. The wallet or purse is second most important because it contains all types of sensitive information. The most sensitive types of information are the identification cards and the social security cards. These two things can initiate all types of fraudulent and deviant behavior. For instance, most ID cards contain the name, address, and distinguishing characteristics of a person like height, weight, hair and eye color. I always try and tell people that revenge is one of the sweetest and at the same time, most evil things in this world. If a person in an adulterous relationship has in any way hurt or dissatisfied the person they are involved with, there are plenty of things the unhappy person can do with an ID card to get even. Here's an example: most of the people with very good to excellent credit are proud of that fact and will usually do anything in his or her power to keep their credit in its present position. What everybody does not know is that the more you apply for credit, the more your credit score is adversely affected. A person can take your information and run rampant, applying for every card they can find. Imagine what that will do to a credit score after about sixty or seventy online applications. And what if the person who has stolen your information applies for and gets sixty or seventy new cards in your name and goes on the shopping spree from hell, with no intention of paying for whatever he or she orders. A person can also jot down the information on your ID to find you just in case you want to prematurely end the relationship by not coming back or not calling after a wonderfully orgasmic week or month of non stop sex. A lot of pregnant women or women who are trying to get pregnant will attempt to procure an ID card for that same reason. They will tell someone 'I can't get pregnant' (by the way if you fall for that, you're either deep in love or a complete jackass!) or 'I'm on birth control' or 'I'm using the patch, whatever. Then when these little lying asses do get pregnant, the fool who got them that way can do nothing but say damn! Anyway, many of the people who involve themselves in affairs are smart enough to keep their kids out of that relationship but many of those smart people also carry pictures of their families in their wallets and purses. Pictures normally would not be anything to raise an eyebrow over but they do silently connect a cheater to his or her family. No one ever really knows what's on the mind of another person. No one knows the mental stability or mental instability of anyone else. No one knows how a person will react when they are hurt or threatened. What if you as a cheater, whether intentionally or unintentionally, severely hurt the person you are having an affair with? What's to stop them from going after someone in your family, especially kids? General conversation between a cheater and the person he is cheating with can divulge more information that what's necessary or advised. A woman, for instance, can say 'I'm looking for a good school to send my child. What school does your son go to?' Then, all they would need to do is ask to see pictures of your kids or sneak a peek into the wallet while you're in the bathroom or sleeping. Once a person knows what your children look like, how hard would it be for them to travel to the school under the guise of a coworker and make up some lie about the parents having been involved in some kind of accident, just to have the child released into their custody. This may frighten some people but every school in the world is not as diligent with its guardian screening measures as we would hope. I can speak from personal experience when I say that I have walked into a school that I have never set foot in before and said I'm here to pick up my girlfriend's child and was given the child. Now the fact that the child recognized me was probably helpful on the part of the school but what if I had just killed my girlfriend – these people are just allowing me to walk out of the school with this child to do whatever debauchery to him I please. Now please understand that I do not consider myself to be a crazy individual or one who has psychotic tendencies, but what if someone else who knew the child was crazy or did have those psychotic tendencies? You can threaten them, maybe even beat the living shit out of them behind the thought but if they accomplish their ultimate goal, which is hurting you, who suffers more? Remember, if people can't get at you directly, they will use the indirect route. The indirect route usually consists of family, assets, then character. Look at the mindset of someone who cheats. Whether on a test or in a relationship, they are trying to take the easy way out by doing something deceptive. For those of you who are computer literate, ask yourselves, how hard is it to take a scanner and copy the image off the ID card then transfer that image to the ID card of someone else. If a person has your ID, credit card and social security number, they can go online and buy everything in sight. Certain retailers will allow customers to apply for instant credit. If someone has your information and their picture, your good credit is as good as gone. Keys are the third most important things you should make sure you always take with you. Depending on the mindset of the person you are dealing with, they can do a number of things with your keys. First, if you decide to have an evening at their place or somewhere of their choosing and you mention to them that nature of your visit is a one night stand, if they like you, they may hide your keys from you thereby forcing you to eventually return for a second night stand. This most often works with married people or those living together. Here's how; when people live together, nine times out of ten, both parties have keys to the home. If one party is cheating, and the method above is employed, the cheating party will go home and tell the significant other that he or she has lost their keys somewhere. Meanwhile the other person involved in the affair will hide the keys from the married or committed party until they either feel like giving them back or until they make copies. Second, if they are crazy and you are dumb enough to let them know where you live, they or someone they know could be prompted to pay you an unexpected visit – especially if you have hurt them. They can also copy your car keys, go joyriding with your vehicle while you're at work or depending upon your job, they can enter into sensitive areas and do the ungodly.

Remember, being good takes little planning. Being good is an extension of the blueprint instilled in most people by their righteous, law-abiding parents. Being bad is something people often have to work on. It is something most people need to practice or perfect. Holding a door for somebody or helping a person with a heavy object does not take much thought. It is almost instinctive. When someone does something bad, for instance hurting another, there is at least the initial thought, followed by the hurtful action. Sometimes there is also the thought of what may happen after the action but that thought is usually dismissed. When a person gets to the point where being bad comes easy or 'natural' therapy is usually in order. Simply put to avoid getting caught in the practice of infidelity, people must become exceptionally good at being exceptionally bad.

Chapter Three
Complete Trust – Goal Or Fallacy

One of the worst things in the world is having a romantic involvement with someone you can't trust. The constant nagging in your mind which is often confused with insecurity, the always wanting to ask 'who's that?' when your significant other talks to another on the phone or acknowledges someone of the opposite sex and most disturbing, the 'I wonder who he or she is with when they're not with me.' Trust issues are one of the most confusing and most damaging factors in relationships because if you don't confront them, like a childhood bully, the effects can last a lifetime. This means that if a person is involved with someone to whom he or she gives their heart to and this person cheats on him or her, the level of hurt which is experienced may make it impossible for the hurt person to recover. People who experience this kind of hurt are often easy to recognize but not that easy to help when it comes to getting past that hurt. Things that people who have been hurt have in common include the disassociation from others and the internalization of the pain. These people will blame themselves for whatever went wrong in the relationship and this will eventually lead to self esteem issues which will eventually lead to them not wanting to be involved in relationships altogether. Being a giant conspiracy fanatic and victim of several trust destroying relationships, I find that trust is almost non existent when it comes to new people and new relationships. For a while I honestly believed that I was one of only a few people who shared this thought process. I quickly came to realize however that everybody who has been involved in a relationship has been hurt in a relationship. It comes with the territory. But as I mentioned before, it is not so much the fact that people have been hurt as it is the fact of how people get past that hurt. Some people seek assistance from those who can actually help them, like professionals in the relationship field or members of clergy. Some people have chain relationships (one after the other) in an attempt to forget the hurt. Some people even subconsciously hold on to the hurt in an effort to not get hurt again, which will eventually cause more hurt. This all boils down to the level of trust that a person has or is willing to give. The thing about trust is that it is so very fragile. It is easily manipulated. Unless a person has the clearness of conscience and faith in their partner to dismiss any potential doubt which may come about whether from a nosey girlfriend or a jealous best friend, the trust can be blown about the same way a feather would be in a light wind. When people meet for the first time, unless they have done extensive research, they only know about the other person what that other person tells them. In a new relationship, people have to allow themselves to be vulnerable, meaning they will have to take a chance on getting to know someone, hope that they'll like them after they get to know them and hope that they will not turn out to be anything like their ex husband, ex wife, ex boyfriend or ex girlfriend. To talk about vulnerability for a second, many people do not realize that it can be manipulated for a person's benefit. When a couple breaks up, both parties go through a period of vulnerability, meaning they may get involved with someone else prematurely to circumvent the feelings of loneliness and unhappiness, which may remain. In simplified terms this means a person may sleep with someone else right after he or she breaks up just because they need to fill that void. This person is the rebound lover. Chances are a relationship formed during this time will rarely last. A person who just wants a relationship, physical or otherwise may 'sympathize' with someone else who is genuinely hurt to make him or her believe that he or she actually cares. All a person would have to do is say 'I broke up with my husband or wife too and I don't know how I can make it' for the other person, who is or may actually be hurt to believe them and offer companionship. The real bad down side to distrust, if there is such another downside, is that there is always the possibility that no matter how much evidence you think you have on someone you suspect of wrongdoing, you yourself may still be wrong. Life is funny like that. If you act on your incorrect suspicions and your partner chooses to stay with you, chances are they will never let you live it down, the fact that you incorrectly accused them of wrongdoing or if they do let you live it down, they will never forget. When a person has doubt about the fidelity of their partner, they will often look for things. They will play Part Time Private Eye in the hopes that they will catch their partner doing something derogatory. They will ask their best friends to corroborate unreliable evidence in the hopes that the best friends will back up the suspicious person's suspicions. In any type of relationship, there has to be at least a basic level of trust. The type of relationship a person has with his or her significant other will determine how high the level of trust goes. What happens though in too many relationships is that the trust which should be there is replaced by concern for one's own feelings. The 'I trust you but…' or the 'I would commit to you if only…' That little iota of uncertainty, which has been caused by past relationships, does not always leave when a relationship goes sour. Many times the uncertainty will bring its luggage and settle into a person's heart, preventing that person from ever being able to fully distance themselves from past hurt. The idea of complete trust is a wonderful thing. Knowing that you can tell your partner anything, knowing that your partner will be there for anything and through anything is a feeling, which cannot easily be matched. However, many times this feeling is similar to the new relationship euphoria as well as new relationship sex, meaning it is absolutely fabulous in the beginning but will only last for a certain amount of time. How many people in this world can truly say they know their partners so well, they have achieved that level of unconditional and complete trust where another person or a misunderstood situation cannot cause doubt? I don't believe many. Unconditional love means loving through uncertainty. It means loving through infidelity. It means being able to love through whatever life throws at you. People throw the word unconditional around all the time especially at weddings. Yet at the first sign of trouble, as in finding out your life partner has given you a venereal disease, people head for the hills. Now granted, getting a sexually transmitted disease from someone who supposedly 'loves' you is very much disheartening, damaging and just plain bad and many people in this world don't believe you should be forced to remain in a relationship with that person but what those people don't completely understand is that this is the very type of thing unconditional love entails. This is one of those situations, which resembles infidelity. A person could have had a pre-existing condition, which shows no symptoms or shows commonly mistakable symptoms for years. (Like certain types of sexually transmitted diseases) A person would have to trust that the other person is not lying and is just as surprised as their partner. While some married people believe commitment starts at the first sexual experience, some married people believe that commitment does not actually start until the actual wedding and some people even believe that commitment begins once a couple begins dating. What if during a bachelor party, as many times is the case, the groom gets a little too drunk and ends up having sex with one of the teenage strippers trying to work their way through college? What if the groom never had sex with anyone else until that night and what if that college student had a sexually transmitted disease, which she gave to the groom and which kept itself hidden till much later in the marriage? The groom under questioning may honestly say I don't know how you got an std because I never cheated on you. If he remembers the bachelor party, he may say also say we weren't married yet, so it doesn't count as me cheating on you. The bride will be left with the option of believing the groom and forgiving him or thinking he cheated and is just using the bachelor party excuse to escape an ass whippin'. Unconditional love means I love you through even the most extreme of circumstances. Worst-case scenario - even if you cause a family member of mine to lose their life, I have to forgive and still love you. Not many people are capable of that. In the simplest of terms, unconditional love means I love you - No Matter What. Unconditional or complete trust is much the same. A person must be able to let go of inhibitions and start each relationship as if it were the first one they have ever been in. This is why a cooling off period between relationships is not only highly suggested but necessary. When people jump into new relationships without even so much as taking a breather from the old, they carry along luggage from the old. Without completely clearing their mind, body and heart of the old person, they sometimes confuse aspects of the old person and the new, which will more often than not ground a relationship before it has a chance to get off the ground. Unconditional trust means I have to trust you even if everybody we both know tells me you're cheating. Unconditional trust means I have to trust you even if I find out you are cheating and I desire to keep you and the relationship going. It doesn't mean being stupid, it means loving & trusting 'in spite of.' It means almost falling into the dreaded realm of complacency. A person cannot be involved in a relationship and say 'I love my partner but I don't trust them.' If so, that person is lying or maybe that person is not exactly lying but definitely involved in a different type of love. AKA I love you as a friend or I love certain things about you - and so on and so forth. This is another way deception can allow cheating to enter into a relationship. A person can force his or her partner to prematurely answer a difficult question by just making a statement, for instance, I love you or I trust you. Most people who say these words expect to hear nothing but the same words repeated back to them and not only do they expect to hear these words repeated back to them – they expect to hear them verbatim. What is not often realized is that trust and love do not enter into or exit a relationship at exactly the same time. People often manipulate the feelings of another by telling them they're in love or they trust them completely, knowing that the partner who probably does not feel the same, will not reciprocate those feelings, for fear of hurting the significant other. Trust is one of the main components of love and not the type of love a person has for their co-workers or neighbors but the type of love shared between two people that no other can come between, the type of love marriages are supposed to be based on. Trust and love in a relationship go hand in hand and it is utterly impossible to maintain one without the other. As I mentioned earlier, there are different levels of trust and those levels are determined by what type of relationship a person has. In my experience, I have noticed three main levels of trust. A dating type of relationship is what I like to call the level one type of trust. This relationship is basic, meaning there's trust but not so much that if its bond was broken, one would not be able to recover. There is not that much trust in this type of relationship because it is generally in the new, formative stage and the heart is not completely involved as in that of a boyfriend and girlfriend relationship. Level two is what I like to call the boyfriend & girlfriend type of relationship. This relationship has more trust than level one because there is a certain stratum of commitment. The heart is involved but there is no long term promise of fidelity and if there are no kids involved, the length of togetherness will usually only last as long as good times prevail. Level three is the married with children type. I call this level three because it is the most committed and closet to complete trust type of relationship I have experienced. People who fall into this category trust their partners to take care of their kids, to come home to them every night, to support them emotionally, financially and physically but they know that there's always the possibility of them failing due to the human factor - human factor being that they will eventually tire of one another or simply fall out of love. I find complete trust is nothing more than a plateau people shoot for much like perfection. People desire the idea, yet are unfamiliar with the concept. This type of trust has shown to be as elusive as Santa Claus. Sure you may see a lot of bearded, fat white men dressed in red & white suits during the holiday season but if you look closely, you will realize they are not the real thing, just a personification of the idea. When you honestly think about it, who over the age of about five really believes reindeer fly? Who really has seen a jolly man sneaking into people's chimneys without getting arrested or shot? Much in common with complete trust, you often see what it resembles, yet has anyone ever seen the real thing? I for one sure haven't. Complete, unconditional and unequivocal trust, just like Santa Claus or the idea of, few people in this world actually believe it exists.

Chapter Four
The Commitment Trap

One of the worst things in this world besides having a romantic involvement with someone you can't really trust is having a romantic involvement with someone you don't really like. I'm sure some of you may be asking how is it even possible to be involved with someone and not have an attraction to that person. That is a very valid question because it is almost impossible to do. Every person involved in a relationship has been attracted to the other person in some way, shape or form – no matter how miniscule. What I am speaking of however is a romantic involvement, which is possible on so many different levels. People in relationships today have motivations, which can stretch from financial to parental to actual love. Some of these relationships can be asymmetrical - meaning one person can be in it only to satisfy his or her desires. They can also be symmetrical – meaning each person works equally to satisfy the other. If one person in a relationship is rich beyond the other's wildest dreams, the not so rich person may act as if there's actual love but there needn't be. If a relationship exists where children are involved, some people who only wanted children may act as if there is a romantic interest as well but again there needn't be. Surprisingly, there are a few relationships, which involve actual love but there are many more, based solely on sex, which are giving the 'love' ones one helluva run for their money. There is a popular saying, which has been around for about as long as I can remember and which describes some of the deception surrounding men and women. It goes 'women fake orgasms, men fake relationships.' When you think about it, this saying is more than just true because men, no matter how much they lie about it, are rarely able to tell if a woman has an actual orgasm during the act of intercourse. The woman may act as if she is climaxing and she may tell the man 'yes, yes, oh yes' when he asks but other than that, how many men can really tell? The disheartening fact for many women is that few of them actually achieve orgasm during the act of sex. The reasons why women do not reach their point as often as men do vary from inadequate stimulation to psychological issues and beyond but the fact still remains. Many men are aware of this fact but do not think it applies to them. They often think that just because a woman says yes, yes, yes, she is totally and undeniably satisfied. Women, on the other hand, are rarely able to tell if a relationship is actually that or in laymen's terms, if a man is 'faking it.' Just like the men, these women feel that if things are not going 'bad' as what is defined by most of society, then the relationship is 'good' and in fact an actual relationship. What makes it easy to fake a relationship is the fact that when it comes to the bad things, they usually include arguing, cheating and general unhappiness. When there is a fake relationship, a person will do whatever is necessary to not do any of the above. Men and women have both faked relationships but historically, males have been known to start and continue these relationships without usage of their hearts. It's clearly understandable that people do not want to involve themselves totally in a relationship because they fear being used but a lot of men will not give all of themselves ever. A lot of people are involved today in what are called <u>appearance unions.</u> This means they basically do what makes them happy and what makes people outside the relationship assume their relationship is going well. For instance, a man may not like a certain woman due to her beliefs or her attitude or whatever but because the satisfying of his sexual urges makes every other aspect of the relationship tolerable, he will stay in a relationship with her – or a couple may be in the public eye and their relationship is only together because to part would be financially detrimental to one or both. In regard to the above statement about men and women, I wouldn't exactly say men fake relationships as much as I would say they have relationships with women's body parts. Ever notice how some men will only talk to a woman if her body fits into a certain "frame"? These men will gawk at women, stare them up and down, undress them with their eyes to make sure these women are a perfect 34-28-36 or whatever measurements tickle these men's fancy. Some people classify it as ogling and more and more people are gaining acceptance of it. Even though a high number of men indulge in it and a high number of women for some reason or other think it's flattering, I don't believe a relationship should be based on or started because of it. In my second book, Relationships, pacification for crazy people, I tried to figure out the attraction, rather the compulsion, which drew people toward certain relationships. Through many acquaintances, I found that dependency was a heavily contributed factor. I found more relationships consisting of 'I want what you can do for me' rather than 'I want you just because.' I also found many, many relationships falling under the 'I'm independent, I want you to be independent also but we have to be independent together' umbrella. This, from most accounts would not be considered a bad thing since independence is something we as human beings are all born with. It's just that what people don't always realize is that everybody in this world is dependent on someone for something or other, especially in a relationship. Trying to maintain independence in a relationship is one of the hardest things to do thanks to the unwritten and expected compromising statute. This statute states that people are knowingly and willingly supposed to give up things they enjoy for the relationship's existence and betterment. These joys and freedoms are given up by both sides for peace in the relationship because it is almost impossible for someone to become involved with another and not change at all and have the relationship be a happy one. Here's an example; certain people love the club scene, yet when two people who love the club scene get together and start a family, their love for that type of atmosphere must change for a successful or at least continued relationship. Think about it; clubs are historically and notoriously known for being prime places to meet the opposite sex. Almost everybody who meets and hooks up with someone he or she met in a club will more than likely believe that that person they met will continue to meet and possibly hook up with other people at clubs if that person were to go out alone - not to mention if a family is actually started, there will be very little time for either of the parties to actually enjoy shaking his or her behind. Now don't get me wrong, there are many people who can easily shirk their responsibilities and enjoy doing so at a moment's notice but some part of the relationship will experience unhappiness if this were to happen. If the club pattern was to continue, meaning one or both still enjoyed the partying after starting a family as much as they did before the family was started, somewhere down the line the family life would definitely suffer. It would suffer because either one of the two would feel neglected or the child or children would feel neglected by the parents. This is where you sometimes get grandmas and grandpas or even neighbors and best friends raising babies. People don't always understand how their activities affect others. In the example above both people could be pure of heart individuals just looking for a good time. The more time they spend away from each other however, the more chance suspicion has to sneak in. Before the couple gets together, a woman could go to a club every week and see the same guy she is interested in each time and think 'he's just here doing the same thing I am, having a little fun.' But after a connection is made and possibly a family is started, the woman could be thinking 'we're a couple or we're a family now - I don't go to the club anymore, neither should he.' If there is no compromise on the amount of going out, the woman may go out one day and say 'I'm a good, honest person. I just go to the club to dance and relieve some parenting tension. But the idea of the man she is involved with doing the same can make the thoughts leap from 'he's just going out to have a good time and relieve some workday tension also' to 'that no good bastard is going to the club looking for ass!' This comes about simply because trust is many times expected to grow at the same rate for one as it is expected to grow for the other. In many relationships like the one above, if the woman stops going to the club because she has a man, then automatically the man is supposed to stop going because he has her and if he doesn't that is when the suspicion and distrust will set in. The trust issue is one major thing people in relationships need to constantly monitor but combine it with inadequate or improper parenting and you have a definite recipe for disaster. Single people for example or should I say the perpetually happy don't always realize that when relationships solidify, changes are eminent. Some changes are temporary. Some are lifelong. Some people call the acceptance of these changes maturing. Other people call it losing independence and still others call it the beginning of the end. Coming to the realization that you can't go and just boink your ex because your present partner doesn't want to have sex is part of it. Another part of it is realizing that your feelings are not always going to be put first. Some people call this losing happiness. Some people call it finding happiness.

Maybe it's just a different kind of happiness. Who knows? Anyway, I titled this chapter the commitment trap because commitment, when used by some people is nothing more than a form of entrapment. It is almost the equivalent of undercover law enforcement officers breaking the law in front of suspected criminals in the hopes that they will follow behind and break the law as well. People have forgotten that commitment or the idea of is supposed to be mutual, where both parties <u>desire</u> being in a relationship with one another. Commitment is not contractual nor is it the work of some crafty magician in high heels and a blue dress. A commitment is a promise of exclusiveness. Some people will hype the idea of commitment up so much to sell it to some unsuspecting individual that that particular individual may think there is nothing that can possibly go wrong in the relationship if he or she were to become involved. This is the trap. The best way to understand this is to look at the various and most common types of traps. There's the bear trap. There's the mousetrap and there's the female trap. The bear trap is self-explanatory. It is a claw like trap designed to catch bears. This heavy metal device does not allow a trapped bear much freedom or comfort. Okay let's skip the political correctness, this trap causes excruciating fucking pain. The setter of the trap pretty much has control over the animal once he has been secured. The mousetrap also needs very little explanation. It is a simple device designed to catch mice. There are two popular types, the wire trap and the glue trap. Neither seems as dangerous or as intimidating as the bear trap but each serves a similar purpose. That purpose being to catch and prevent something from escaping. The female trap is a little different because instead of catching a female, this trap is the female. This trap works so well because women know many men cannot think sensibly while certain emotions and or body parts are being stimulated. It is called a trap because as long as the pleasure exists, many men will not leave. These men have the freedom and capability to at any time make their exit, however the level of pleasure combined with the men's immorality is what keeps them. The commitment trap is similar to the previous three but unlike the bear or the mousetrap, the commitment trap does not use a painful consequence as a way of accomplishing its goal and unlike the female trap, the commitment trap does not force its hypnotic influence on anyone. The commitment trap is something many people willingly or unsuspectingly fall into, similar to a gigantic pit covered with tree branches, which for some reason or another these people are unable to escape. It is called a trap because just like love & trust, the desire for commitment usually does not start with both parties at the exact same time. As I mentioned in the beginning of this chapter, the one thing people in relationships still don't realize is that a person can be with you in a relationship but not love you. A person can also love you but not or never as much as you love them. Some people who fall into the commitment trap are just like mice that get caught by a glue trap. They're in a relationship and they're stuck. Movement is restricted. This glue trap type of relationship is not as painful as the wire trap kind but like the wire trap, over time the relationship will become detrimental to one's existence. Feelings of restriction, like the mousetrap, can lead to being in a rut. A rut can lead to depression. People who get caught up in the commitment trap do so because commitment makes itself seem so appealing and necessary. Commitment disguises itself to fool people into believing that without it, they will never be happy. Certain types of commitment can make a person feel that the other is so dependent upon them that if they were to ever leave, the first person would not be able to maintain, which may make that person feel as if they are trapped in the relationship. Commitment is sometimes inviting like the cheese on the wire trap, which tempts the mouse. Commitment is powerful and fast, like the bear trap, where a person may feel as if he or she were set up. Commitment is intriguing and much desired like the female trap often is. Just like there are different kinds of traps, there are different kinds of commitments. They all however have one thing in common. They are all designed to capture and or keep their intended prizes. People will use whatever weapons they have at their disposal to keep another in a relationship or commitment. Children, especially babies are the most sought after methods people use to trap others into relationships. In case any of you are unaware, here are two popular ways this is done. The first is the ole 'I didn't think I could get pregnant' and the second is the 'make junior like him or her so that the conscience of the person you are courting will not let him or her leave the relationship after he or she is already in it for fear of hurting junior.' I know it's not morally right to lie or use children to trap others into relationships but people do it every single day. It's done so much that it astounds me that everybody who has not been trapped by these methods doesn't already know about them.

Here's a question worth pondering; ever wonder why kids don't like broccoli or spinach or basically things, which are good for them - but love the hell out of ice cream and candy, things, which are notoriously not good for them? I like to think it's because parents never give the same kind of introduction to broccoli and spinach the way they do ice cream. Ice cream and candy, besides always being associated with fun times, almost always have an 'ooh yummy' beginning. Isn't it funny how you never hear of anybody other than Popeye going ga ga over broccoli or spinach? By the same token, you never hear anybody saying 'eat your ice cream so you can have spinach.' Parents unwittingly make ice cream and candy so appealing that kids have no choice but to like it. At the same time however, they make the other foods, which do not taste as well seem like they are not as good for them as they actually are. Granted, people are always going to have different tastes when it comes to food but when you help them along by saying yuk or yum, those people will either hate or like something that much more. Commitment is made to seem appealing just like the ice cream, whether through happy wedding pictures or gazillion dollar rings. Cheating is always fun and exciting. Commitment, after a period of time, is not. The one major difference behind these two is that cheating, no matter when it occurs, always evokes a measure of excitement, due to the possibility of capture. Commitment, unless consistently concentrated on will lead to monotony. Almost everyone knows that doing the same thing or doing the same person will eventually get boring. Nobody likes to be bored. This is one of the basic reasons why many people try to trick or trap others into commitments.

Chapter Five
Methods To Cheat

This is the one chapter everybody who has had a successful adulterous liaison claims to be an expert on. These people feel that since they haven't been caught cheating, they know better about infidelity than everyone else who has. Now granted, while a person may know quite a bit about infidelity, what's not always known and what is often overlooked is the fact that when a person gets caught doing something wrong, that is the time they often realize their mistake(s). For instance, when some people go to jail, many times they come out knowing more about the crime that sent them there than when they first went in. These people also know almost as much about the legal process as a lot of first year attorneys. When a person commits a transgression, if they are successful, often they will find themselves placed in what's commonly called a false sense of security. This sense of security exists because that person may think that since no one has outright accused or confronted them, they have gotten away with whatever it was they were trying to get away with. They don't realize that all people are not the impulsive type who will jump out and say AHA! at the precise moment a transgression takes place. There are some people who will watch you, let you get away with the small stuff until the time is right, then spring the trap. This is what law enforcement does all the time. They will let the street level drug dealers off with a slap on the wrist in the hopes they will eventually return to their criminal activity and eventually lead them to the bigger fish. When a person cheats, depending on what type of relationship they have or depending upon the time invested into the relationship, their partner may immediately confront them with the evidence, respond with the revenge tactic (my favorite) or let evidence build for an absolutely fantastic and undisputable climax. As I mentioned in my first book, The Correct Way To Fool Around, the idea of cheating is not something, which should be taken lightly, if that is what you plan to do. Catching a person in an adulterous act has led to some extreme consequences, least of which being separation. People have lost homes, entire families, even lives due to a single act of infidelity. This is why it is of utmost importance that if you plan to do this, you must leave no room for error. Remember, the simplest crime should take a year of planning. People who are under the illusion of invincibility because they have yet to get caught are just that – under a cloud of illusion. The longer a person remains in any type of negative situation, the longer they have to be noticed or caught. In short, their time of judgment has yet to come.

To be successful at cheating, a person generally needs three things, opportunity, a willing partner and common sense. *Opportunity* is one of, if not the most important ingredient needed when it comes to partaking in infidelity. What's so remarkable about opportunity is that unlike when relating to a job, opportunities for infidelity always seem to knock at precisely the right time. Turmoil in the relationship, unchallenged suspicions and sexual neglect are all things, which invite infidelity. Backed up rent and past due bills, on the other hand, require but do not invite a job. Opportunity is basically the right time combined with the right place. Places do not have to be extravagant and times can vary like the wind but they both must be mutually acceptable for an affair to take place.

A willing partner is a given - you can't cheat by yourself unless you're talking about Internet pornography and that's not what I genuinely like to call cheating as much as an immoral hobby or unless you're talking about Ms. Palmer or Mr. Finger. A willing partner is someone who resides on the same mental, emotional and physical level as you. Someone who, in a losing battle with his or her conscience, will not go and tell your partner you're being unfaithful. A willing partner is someone who has to be able to keep secrets, as well as someone who is able to differentiate and separate feelings of ecstasy and love.

Common sense is something everyone in this world, not just cheaters, needs to have. Common sense, not to the extent of Thomas Paine's work in the 18th century but just the knowledge that at a certain age a person should be aware of certain things, is so elusive because too many people think that other people in this world are just not as smart as they themselves are. This is the thinking shared by many a philanderer and also one of the main reasons why many cheaters get caught. Cheaters often become lax in their efforts to hide their indiscretions because they (1) have gotten away with them for so long and (2) after a certain amount of time, feel their partners just don't care to be as diligent in trying to catch them as they may have been in the past. The one thing about common sense, which is unfortunate, is that there is no set amount, which the world can use as a gauge to determine sensibility for certain actions. And as we all know, common sense is quite often a contradiction in terms. What some people overlook is what some other people find. This statement is not rocket science but a perfect example of the elusive 'common logic' or 'common sense.' When new or expectant parents 'babyproof' or 'childproof' their homes, they do so by looking through the eyes of a child. This can include getting down on hands & knees, checking and locking cabinets and securing everything a young child's curiosity would probably cause them to have access to. When a person cheats however, they need to 'wifeproof' or 'husbandproof' their homes also but they rarely do. Now even though I am an extremely big advocate of not using the home to cheat, some people feel they can accomplish this secretly and successfully and to those people I wish an emphatic 'Good luck!' Remember, neighbors see everything! As I mentioned before, people not only need to adult proof their residences but they need to do so by looking through the eyes of their significant other. The immediate question on their minds should be 'if I were my wife or husband and they suspected me of cheating, what would I look for?' To become proficient at this, one must understand what the opposite sex has a propensity for losing. For instance, women wear many different hairstyles and some of those hairstyles require the use of hairpins. If a man is cheating and his wife does not have the amount or style of hair, which would require hairpins, why would they be in the house or more specifically why would they be in the bed? Men have a history of being forgetful. Whether it's a case of selective amnesia or an actual medical condition, men are famous for forgetting. Things high on the forgetful list include keys, cell phones and watches. These things are usually small and with the exception of the watch, can be unisex items. What can get a woman in trouble is if they are questioned by their husband regarding if anyone stopped by and they say no, then the left behind cell phone rings or the keys or watch is found. These are small, usually overlooked things, which can lead to an argument, which can lead to divorce. I doubt if there is a cheater who hasn't been caught or suspected due to a misplaced condom wrapper or because they let someone use their husband or wife's brush. These are common, rookie mistakes. Rookie mistakes, no matter how common or insignificant, will get you hurt. Attention to detail and not just the regular kind but extreme scrutiny of certain issues will lessen the likelihood of you getting caught. For the people who are not as brazen as the ones above, don't cheat in your own home unless you live by yourself and even then keep the affairs to a minimum because the more people you cheat with, the more chance you have of one of them returning at an inopportune time. Inopportune meaning while you're with hubby or wifey. It won't matter how much you tell a person not to call or come back to your place of residence if they are 'whipped' by your loving. If I may suggest something, always use a different hotel. Using a hotel will eliminate the need for searching, finding and cleaning up wet spots. It will also alleviate the concern over a missed or forgotten condom. The bad thing about hotels is that unlike someone's home, if a person were to lose a valuable or sentimental item like say an engagement or wedding ring the chances of it being found in a timely manner like before the significant other realizes its missing, are severely lessened. A different hotel should be used each time because when a person does the same thing, he or she develops a pattern. Some people pick up on patterns rather quickly. All it would take is for Ryan to be spotted going into or coming out of the Horny Hyena Hotel on two consecutive Saturday nights with Kim for the connection to be made and the air of suspicion to be raised. Spontaneity is one of the things people need and not just to keep the romance alive in their relationships but also to keep from getting caught in the act of infidelity. When people do the same thing, it gets boring, routine and if done in public, noticed. Many couples with kids often have what's called a weekend whoo hoo or Saturday night sex party. This allows the kids to get out of the house and the parents to get their freak on. This is great but as I said before it becomes routine and expected. What happens if a change in one partner's schedule occurs and Saturday nights are no longer an option? That couple will have to go and plan a new getaway night from the kids, which depending on available daycare or night care may be somewhat difficult. When infidelity is planned, many participants follow a routine. They either go to the same places or go to different places but at the same times – as in every Thursday at seven. This is bad because **anybody** with half an ounce of common sense or intellect will be able to put two and two together and realize 'hey something is going on here.' What people who don't want to get caught in the act of infidelity should do is use their brains to be spontaneous and by this I do not mean every week call up your partner and say 'hey let's go to a new hotel' or 'let's take your car today.' I mean do something creative such as mailing a note or letter to your natural partner's residence or job inviting then to a real estate seminar or something along those lines. The reason I say mail is because many people who are suspected of being involved in an adulterous union are often unaware of that fact and sometimes have significant others who go through great lengths to catch them – some going so far as to put a tap on the phone or even setting up hidden video in the home. There are many Internet companies, which offer email as well as keystroke recording. These companies have computer programs, which will record every email received as well as every keystroke made on your computer. Perfect for those looking to catch their significant others in an online affair. Technology is moving at an incredible rate and for every advancement, there really seems to be a way to counter it. One of the things people often overlook is how efficient some of the old technology actually still is. Few people other than prison guards and those expecting terrorist activity actually monitor snail mail. When it comes to the mail, most people receive a good portion of what's known as junk mail. This includes offers to change phone service, offers to participate in multi level marketing business ventures and let's not forget the ever popular time share vacation promotion. Most of the people in this world just overlook these items when they arrive, then throw them out. But if a particular piece of correspondence is expected, the intended party will know just what to look out for. This of course brings out the problem of addressing the envelope. Most of the solicitation offers either comes addressed to a particular person or to current resident. What a person can do for instance is send an invitation to a seminar to the person he or she is cheating with and then meet up with them at the seminar, sit together like they don't know each other, pretend to get bored and leave – to go wherever and to do whatever. (Leave separately of course!) This brings about the problem of the inside of the envelope. If you get one of these invitations to go to one of those dreadfully boring, money making seminars, you can open the envelope, remove the information, repack the information into a brand new envelope, address the envelope with the name and residence of the person you are already or planning to sleep with, go to a post office outside of your neighborhood and send it to him or her. Two things you must remember; one, most people throw away junk mail, so you must do something that will make the intended party know that it's from you. This can be done by using a nickname or a middle initial, which is not the person's actual. Let's say you are dealing with a woman named Leslie J. Williams. What you could do is address the envelope to read Leslie B. Williams. Anyone else in the household who may nosey around the mail when that particular piece of correspondence arrives will probably think that it was an honest mistake on the part of the sender. Leslie J. Williams however will know better. The second thing you must remember is the more professional something appears, the less that thing will be scrutinized. You can make the envelope appear more professional by buying a rubber stamp with the name and address of Leslie J. Williams. The reason this will work as well as it probably would is because who would actually think a person would ever go to such great lengths just to commit infidelity? Remember the simplest crime should take a year of planning. Another way the envelope could be addressed is by using those little handy dandy pre addressed stickers. This is beneficial for the envelope as well as for the inside of the letter. If the sticker on the inside of the letter idea does not look official or legitimate enough, you can always use a scanner to copy and edit the letter you have. One final thing, don't worry about putting a sender's address on the envelope, many of these solicitors never do! The good thing about this method is that it could be used again and again and again. The bad thing about this is that because you are tampering with the mail, you are quite possibly looking at a federal offense which means federal time. I know you law abiding citizens who have purchased my book have done so only for academic study and would never ever think about doing something illegal - no matter how well it works, right??? Remember there is no limit to the amount of deception in this world.

    <u>Always cheat with somebody who has as much to lose as you do.</u> Someone who is married or someone who has a very close and public relationship with their children make perfect candidates if you want to lessen the possibility of your potential transgression being uncovered. Nine times out of ten, these people hold their relationships in very high regard, even if they are not completely happy in them. More times than not they will risk losing you rather than risk losing the respect of their significant others as well as losing their significant others. Again, I am not instructing anybody to go out and commit adultery and possibly ruin somebody's entire life. This piece of advice is for those of you who already have your hearts dead set on cheating or for those of you using this for academic study. People who are not on equal levels - meaning one person has their own place of residence whereas the other does not or one person has a steady job while the other is habitually unemployed would not make good candidates as far as acceptable cheating partners. Don't misunderstand me, a person can always meet someone in a club and take them home for a one-night fling but to alleviate the chances of getting caught, these people are ones you

should steer clear from – unless it's <u>actually</u> and <u>only</u> a one night stand. Many times that one night stand gets kinda good and the next thing you know that one night stand is staying for breakfast, coming over for the weekend and or causing more drama than what should have been allowed. That is not a one night stand, that is a relationship. The fact that many of these so called one night stands cause so much drama is because rarely do we get to know anything about them other than their measurements coupled with the fact that they want to have sex as much as we do. We live in what's called a take advantage society. Weaker and less educated individuals get taken advantage of all the time. People take advantage of the fact that one person may have more than another and may use that fact to blackmail or coerce them into getting what they want. The fact that the people who attempt blackmail and other acts of coercion have nothing to lose makes it that much easier for them to manipulate the direction of a relationship, cheating or otherwise. If a person lives with his or her parents or lives with friends and is involved in a 'natural' relationship with a married person who has their own apartment, car, etc. a lot of times that single person wouldn't think twice about screwing that other person over by threatening to tell the husband or wife if they want something. The something can be money, more sex or a long-term future with the married person. More times than not, the single person knows that the married person will do everything in their power to keep from losing their husband or wife.

This method maybe classified as a little extreme but then again one must ask are there really any boundaries on deception? If you're in a 'natural' relationship and you are tired of always sneaking around, keeping everything in the dark, introduce your natural partner to your significant other as a long lost family member from out of state. This takes a bit of planning so attention to detail is crucial. Once your natural partner has a clear understanding of your family tree, meaning you have taught them the names of your mom, dad, cousins, etc. have them come over one day with a packed bag or two, when your significant other is at your home. What will be more convincing would be to have an actual bus or plane ticket on the bag or in the person's possession. This does not mean that your natural partner has to get on a plane or bus just for that purpose but it will help. I've noticed that certain bus companies have route destinations into almost every town and those that don't very often have destination stops in neighboring towns. What you could do is either take a day trip to a neighboring town and get the baggage claim ticket or just hang out in the bus station and ask someone who has recently arrived for theirs. Once you are able to procure a ticket or other piece of travel evidence, tear off and discard any part, which states the destination or point of origin. It may cost you a few bucks if you try the second strategy and there is always the possibility of police involvement but persistence overcomes resistance. If you are not the type that craves public interaction, computers are your next best option. You can simply go online to any of the major flight or bus carriers, book a small trip and print out a ticket ahead of time for your proposed rendezvous. If that fails or you don't feel like spending the money, you can always use some design software to design a ticket and then go to a print shop to procure some adhesive labels. You then take your artwork, apply it to the labels, apply the labels to your overnight bag and you're done! It would be extremely helpful to confirm that the schedule you are going through all of this trouble to lie about is a schedule, which is actually in effect. Once your natural partner has met your husband or wife, have them tell the story of how they got kicked out of their apartment due to non-payment of rent or due to a very violent breakup. Have them say they have nowhere else to go and they lost your number so they could not call ahead of time. They did however remember your address and just took a chance on you still living there. Only cold hearted bitches will put a family member out on the street with no place to go. If you decide to go with the eviction story, it would be helpful to be very computer literate to create fraudulent documents so as to add credibility to your story. If you decide to go with the broken relationship story, make sure you have an out of state number, which is disconnected or have a 'relative' out of state who will corroborate your story. Someone who will gladly lie and say something like 'that's right, I threw that motherfucker out and he ain't never coming back!' This way your significant other will be aware that you have someone of the opposite sex living in the house but they will be ignorant to the fact that you are screwing their brains out every so often. Ain't deception a mother?

Another tool, which will help greatly in the infidelity game, is what I like to call The Fairy Tale Locator List. Here's how it works: You will need to compile a fairy tale route to keep handy just in case your significant other ever questions you about your whereabouts. By fairy tale route, I mean the residences & businesses along a particular street. Make a small but thorough record of which store follows which and what's on the other side of the street. This is very important because if your significant other is the type to question most or all of your activities away from them, they may ask you to pinpoint your exact location. For instance, if you find yourself on one street and your significant other calls you on your cell phone and asks where are you and you tell your significant other you're on another, if they're doubtful, they may ask you which stores are on the block and in which order. If they are not suspicious of your story, they may ask you to verify some piece of information – for instance; 'honey, you're on Main Street, good. I was there yesterday and I saw this brown dress in the window but I didn't have time to price it. Could you go inside and find out how much it is for me?' The next action you undertake will either cause or eliminate suspicion. If you are lying about your whereabouts and are five miles away from where your significant other thinks you are and he or she is on their cell phone waiting for the price on some item, you have but two courses of action. One, say honey, I've got a call coming in on my other line, I'll call you right back. Then turn off the phone until you get to the store or two, pause, stutter or do any number of things, which will give away the fact that you are not where you said you were. Some people have the type of relationship where they divulge every piece of information that is requested by their partner. This list is especially helpful for those types of people. Let's say you tell your significant other you're on Main Street when you're really on Fourth Street. Your significant other may have a photographic image in her head of what Main Street looks like or worst-case scenario, may actually be on Main Street. You on the other hand may have no idea. If the significant other asks what establishment you are in front of and you can't answer to their satisfaction, there's gonna be trouble. Now if you were to pull out your handy dandy, Fairy Tale Locator List, no matter how extensively they were to question you, they would not be able to prove you wrong unless they were at the exact location you said you were - and in a situation like that, where someone would actually be at or near the location where their significant other is, the only advice I can offer is to tell your significant other that you just hailed a cab and left that location. My second piece of advice would be for you to hightail it to the location your significant other presently is or somewhere very close by.

When people are forced to lie unexpectedly, a pause or

a change in voice pattern is often noticed. To counter this, practiced answers to questions, which are likely to arise during an infidelity interrogation (ii) are extremely helpful. As in the case of job interviews, there are hundreds upon hundreds of books, which help a person get ready. These books cover everything from what to say, what not to say, what to wear, what questions are likely to be asked and the proper way to answer them. The reason why many applicants do not obtain their desired position is not because they are unskilled but rather because they fail during the questioning phase of the interview. I remember many years ago applying for a job as a stock clerk. This position was in a very 'ritzy' type of establishment in a very 'ritzy' part of the city, which was probably what contributed to my nervousness. In hindsight I wonder why the hell was I nervous at all. I mean for crying out loud, the job consisted of folding and stacking towels. Not to go off on a rant here but I didn't get the job and I wondered for more than an ample amount of time why. I know the application was filled out correctly, I's dotted and t's crossed and I know I met the experience requirements because there were none. I continued to wonder if the reason was because I stuttered over most of my answers during the interview or could it have been that folding the towels came with some physics type of formula, which only a person with bachelor's degree could unravel? I thought to myself, how fucking hard could it be to fold a towel? I finally settled on the reason for my not being hired as my totally uncomfortable and unprepared state during the interview. What I also realized was that many people talk themselves into or out of a job by giving the right or wrong answers. Case in point, certain security guard supervisors. Note security is one of the simplest jobs ever created. Most jobs entail standing around, looking at either cameras or people. Granted there is a basic level of job knowledge, which one must possess in order to accomplish the job but it's nowhere near rocket science. Too many of these security guard supervisors are hired with little or no on the job experience. They are hired due to either college or life experience which translates into time in service. Again not meaning to go off on a rant but some of these security guard supervisors who get hired without pertinent experience do so mainly because they impressed the hell out of whoever it was that held the interview or because they pay for the job. This gives credence to the fact that some assholes get away with murder or are given certain positions due to how well they talk or how well they bullshit. Anyway, getting back to my original point, in a job interview a question, which is almost always asked, is tell me about yourself. This question does not mean tell the interviewer about your snake collection or your penchant for scratching certain body parts when the weather gets warm. From my experience, 'tell me about yourself' means tell the interviewer about your work history – and nothing else. People often talk themselves out of a job because they divulge more than what's necessary or more than what's asked for. One of the first or biggest questions a person will be asked during an infidelity interrogation (ii) is 'who is that?' if you are on the receiving end of this question and plan to lie about this during an (ii) the worst answer you can give is 'nobody.' The second worst answer you can give is 'oh, that's my friend.' The reason these answers are so bad is because they're the same answers every cheater who doesn't want to divulge more information than they have to, will give. You have to remember that when a suspicious person questions their partner about another person, their level of suspicion is nearing the danger zone. Danger zone being the dreaded argument over suspected cheating. What the person who is asked needs to do is lower that level of suspicion as quickly as possible and the best way to do this is to provide as much information as necessary to pacify the suspicious partner without giving evidentiary facts. This is a double edged sword because the more you lie, the more chance you have of getting caught but the less you say, the more likely they will think you are dodging answers. Instead of saying 'that's my friend' try something like 'that's Michelle from the office.' The 'nobody' and even the 'friend' excuse are beyond played out - meaning they're popular and many times appropriate but even if they're the absolute truth, by themselves, chances are few people will believe them. Lying should be reflexive, meaning you should have every base covered ahead of time. Every question that your partner may ask, have an answer for as in: 'why is she calling at two a.m.' or even 'why is she calling so much?' To answer questions such as these, a person who is cheating could say, we are working on some office related stuff or we are planning a surprise party for her husband. This of course brings about the problem of avoiding the response questions that the innocent spouse will surely have. Some of those questions will be 'what exactly are you working on at the office' or 'when is Michelle's husband's birthday and what are you two planning?' One of the worst case scenario questions could be 'can I come to the surprise party with you?' A person would be up a creek without a paddle if he is unable to sufficiently answer any and all of the innocent party's questions. To avoid these types of questions a person would have to do his or her homework and this entails making up something like an office project ahead of time, one that can be easily adjusted such as a work schedule for everybody in the office. To circumvent the problem of the birthday, all the cheater would have to do is find out the actual birthday of the husband and plan the affair or at least the lie about the affair or the lie about the person involved in the affair around that date. What many people do is lie when questioned and as we all know, this is an essential part of infidelity but many of these people attempt to conjure up lies off the top of their heads and this creates the problem because many of these people are not as proficient as others when this type of venture is called for. This is why practice is necessary. Practice makes perfect – or as close to it as possible. What people do is forget to tell the people they are cheating with that they are not the only ones connected to the telephone number they were given. When a man and woman live together and the man just happens to answer a call from the individual spending time with the female, if that individual is not know to the man, of course there will be suspicions. They may be miniscule concerns or they may be ginormous trepidations but there will be suspicions. When the person spending time with the female calls again and again and the significant other continues to pick up the phone, no amount of 'that's my friend' will suffice. A person of the opposite sex should not be calling the home of a person in a relationship too much. The only exception is if the calls are from a person who is friends of both parties or if the calls are business related and then both parties should be involved. One of the big problems regarding infidelity is that people get too comfortable in their relationships – so much so, that instead of going through the trouble of lying about their transgressions to their partners, they do absolutely nothing to hide the fact that they are cheating but will get mad at the accusation from their partners. They will then try and switch the focus from their actual cheating to making it seem like their partners are incorrectly accusing them and the ones doing the cheating will start arguments based on that.

Banks are always competing for more business. Bank employees are the utmost in customer service, meaning they are notorious for being nice. Next to hospitals and family, banks are about the best alibi I can think of. This method is ideal for people who deal with several different contracts or contractors and requires a cell phone with a prepaid account. The phone doesn't have to be working or turned on for that matter, just its presence and a good speaking voice are all that's necessary. To accomplish, walk into any bank and say you would like to open an account. Most banks deal with new accounts one on one – face to face. When you are in the process of opening your account, place the cell phone to your ear as if you are answering a call. Engage in a quick conversation with yourself, which includes the line 'I'm running low on minutes.' Then say hello, hello as if the phone has run out of airtime and cut your conversation short. Ask the individual handling your account if you may use their phone. When they say yes (chances are they will always say yes) call your significant other and say you have to work at the bank that particular evening and you don't have any idea how late you'll be. If the bank has several floors, as almost all of them do, this will be more to your advantage just in case the significant other tries to come and locate you. Then, while you are with your natural partner, just turn the cell phone off. If your significant other questions you about their inability to get in contact, you can always say there was no reception in the building. This is good because if they try to call you back at the bank, there's a strong chance they will get an automated response, which will prompt them to enter the extension they are trying to contact. This is also good because the address of the particular branch will almost never show up on the caller

ID. The bad part about this is that since you will have your choice of bank branches to lie from, you will have to remember which one you said you were at because people, if they doubt your story, even a little bit, will question you eons later when you probably have forgotten and Heaven help you if you give the wrong answer. The above is an example of the foundation, which needs to be set before you take off on your sexual escapade. The more elaborate the planning, the more positive the result. However, positive and elaborate results are usually only as good as an individual's memory.

Chapter Six
Methods To Detect

Contrary to popular belief, cheaters <u>are</u> criminals and infidelity is not a victimless crime, as many philanderers like to believe. People who commit infidelity are just criminals of a moral law rather than a legal one and just like the majority of apprehended criminals, all of them make mistakes. It's just that the burden of proof, which is on the innocent party, allows these cheaters the freedom to continue with their transgressions. Catching a person in the act of infidelity to me is one of the truly great feelings in this world. Sure it will hurt like hell if your partner is the one you catch in an adulterous affair but the level of relief, the finality of knowing and not wondering, I believe has no equal. Catching somebody in the act of doing something wrong puts that person in a position of power. It gives them the proverbial 'upper hand.' The people who are caught are basically at the mercy of the ones who caught them because the catchers can immediately punish the perpetrators or just let them go and hold whatever it was they were caught doing over their heads for as long as they deem necessary. Some people say the feeling can be best compared to the euphoria contained in new relationship sex, all encompassing and at the same time liberating. When a person, is caught cheating, the roach/mouse effect often applies – meaning just like when a mouse or roach is spotted in the open, there are usually fifty more behind the wall that you don't see. When a person is caught cheating, it's rare that that incident was the first or only one as many cheaters will try to use in their defense. On occasion an act of infidelity may be the first or only transgression when a person is caught but it will usually be a rare occasion. This is why if there is actual doubt or suspicion about a significant other's fidelity, time should be taken and evidence should be gathered.

There are many ways to catch someone in the act of cheating besides catching them with their pants down in the actual act of cheating. As I mentioned earlier, all cheaters make mistakes and aside from looking for everything in chapter five, there are several things a person can do to catch them. The first piece of advice needed when trying to weed out a cheater is what should initially be done when getting involved with someone and that is to get involved using one's head and not one's heart. The head, which we all know is the housing, which contains the brain. The brain is used to make conscious decisions, to use proper judgment and to differentiate right from wrong. The heart, on the other hand is used basically to pump blood. The heart has far too long been given credit as the cause for certain feelings, which it actually has no control over. Feelings, which are generally controlled by the brain, for instance, the sense of touch are connected to the brain but feelings, which show emotion, as in happiness or sorrow are for some reason or another always connected to the heart. (Affairs of the heart, crimes of the heart, etc.) That little fist sized, blood pumping instrument has been so long associated with any type of emotional feeling that whatever goes wrong in a relationship is not due to bad judgment or the inability to get along but a violation of the rules of the heart.

I.E., someone breaks your heart. People who base relationships on the head have a more 'this person will be a good parent for my children or this person will help provide a stable home for us' way of thinking. People who base relationships on the heart have a more 'this person will make pretty children' type of mindset. People who fall into example number one I believe are the hardest to catch because they are more likely to cheat less and think more about the circumstances surrounding the infidelity if in fact they do decide to cheat. People in example number two, since they are usually focused more on the material or physical aspects of a relationship have been shown to be less mindful of attention to detail. A person who follows their head will look for and accept facts as they come. A person who follows their heart may see infidelity clear as day but find ways to make excuses as in 'maybe my husband's pretty young secretary, whose children's picture my husband carries around in his wallet, really does go on business trips with him solely for business.' Now one of the best ways to catch a suspected philanderer, regardless to whether you think with your head or your heart is by setting a trap. The best type of trap is a baited one. Just as one would bait a mousetrap with cheese, the trap for a suspected philanderer should be an attractive member of the opposite sex or of the same sex if the situation so calls. A very successful test or trap – however you want to look at it is the 'make your partner prove their fidelity trap.' This is accomplished by having someone that your partner does not know, come on to them. This task is both easy and difficult. Easy because (1) everybody has friends their partner does not know. (2) Difficult because the decoy you hire may garner an attraction to your partner and cross the line that you had hoped your partner wouldn't. Married members of your family are the best ones to play this role but if you can't conjure up a family member, an old classmate, 'good' friend from out of town or former coworker should do just fine. If you know anybody at the job of the person you suspect, that would be great too because then you could set the foundation by saying to your significant other that you and that person used to live in the same neighborhood or something. Then you could have that person you know tell your significant other something to the effect of how your boyfriend or girlfriend stole their ex or had a one night fling, which was uncovered and it hurt you so much, you've been hell bent on revenge ever since. This may seem a little twisted, so I'll use names to alleviate any confusion. Kim & Ryan are committed. Kim thinks Ryan is fooling around behind her back so she recruits Tasha to check Ryan's fidelity level. Tasha starts flirting with Ryan and lets Ryan know that she was a one time friend of Kim's. Tasha makes up a believable story about how Kim slept with her boyfriend years ago and caused their breakup or how they had a one night stand and Tasha found out about it but did not let Kim know she found out about it. Tasha tells Ryan how much the incident hurt her and how she hasn't been able to get along with her life properly since. This method will allow Ryan the option of saying fair's fair, my girlfriend shouldn't have slept with your ex way back when and anyway Kim's a bitch so she probably deserves getting cheated on – or he could say I'm sorry that happened to you and I feel your pain but I love Kim unconditionally and there's nothing more than an apology either of us can do about it, so scram! The same choices will be afforded to Ryan even if Tasha uses a different method and makes no mention of knowing Kim.

Set 'em up. Some people want to exit a relationship so bad but are for some reason or another unable to. Some of these people are so devious that they will actually make their partners leave them because they are unhappy. One of the ways I've seen this accomplished is by a person setting up their partner to react in a certain manner. After a certain amount of time, people in relationships begin to 'know' their partners. They begin to know how their partners will react to pressure, adversity and or fear. I believe no couple ever completely knows each other but many know their partners well enough to manipulate them based on certain situations. If there's a person in a relationship who will only leave that relationship because of infidelity, the other partner may make it seem like an adulterous act occurred, so that the first partner will either leave the relationship or commit an adulterous act so that the other partner may place blame on them, thereby giving them reason to leave the relationship. Again, so as not to confuse anyone, I'll enlist the help of Kim, Tasha & Ryan. Kim & Ryan are in a supposedly committed relationship but

Ryan desperately wants out. Kim will only leave if Ryan cheats on her. Ryan doesn't cheat and Kim knows this, however he concocts a plan to make Kim believe that he is cheating, even going so far as to make seductive calls to an imaginary person on his cell phone in hearing range of Kim or sending suggestive emails to himself, from a woman's name, which happen to be conveniently left on the screen while Ryan is out of the room. Kim, upon seeing this will more than likely believe that Ryan is definitely cheating and will either leave the relationship or cheat on Ryan. If Kim leaves because she thinks Ryan has cheated, she'll be wrong but Ryan will have accomplished his goal. If Kim cheats on Ryan as a revenge tactic, she'll be wrong again but Ryan can use her infidelity as cause to vacate the relationship, all the while making Kim feel as if she is solely responsible for the breakup. Ain't deception a mother -

Making known the presence of the person who is married but not involved in the affair (the innocent party) has been shown to cause unbelievable turmoil in the world of infidelity. The more people I meet as well as the more cheaters I encounter, it seems I still find people who try and hide their transgressions from their significant others as well as hide their significant others from the other party involved in the affair. In an adulterous relationship, for fear of safety, one should of course hide the fact that they are sleeping around but they should not hide the fact that they are married or in a committed relationship from the person they are involved in the affair with. What I have noticed a great deal of people doing is trying to have 'their cake while being able to eat it too' – meaning they are married, have someone on the side and neither party knows about the other. What this will cause is too much secrecy and often an abundance of unnecessary feelings. Using Kim, Ryan and Tasha again, this is simply a case of Kim and Ryan being married and Ryan cheating on Kim with Tasha. What Ryan is doing wrong, besides cheating, is not informing Tasha that he is married. The extra curricular party, Tasha may feel that the committed party, Ryan is actually pursuing a relationship and this is because the committed party, Ryan never let the extra curricular party, Tasha know that he was married to Kim. Too many people who are involved in affairs try to juggle both relationships secretly. This is extremely difficult to accomplish for some people because many people are not experts at budgeting and basically that is all having two relationships really is – budgeting each relationship equally. What can happen with a person who is not that proficient at budgeting is all three of them may meet up one day and then usually at the most inopportune time, everything will come to a head. Chances are there will be a loud and unnecessary fracas and someone may even end up getting hurt. If you are in a relationship with someone you suspect of cheating and you see that person with a member of the opposite sex or same sex, (depending on your type of relationship) whom you do not know, my suggestion to you is walk right up to the two and introduce yourself and don't introduce yourself the wimpy way as in 'hi sweetheart' then turning to the unknown person and saying, 'hi, my name is Jerry.' Walk right up to your significant other and give them your usual display of affection, whether it be a kiss, hug or whatever, then turn to the unknown person and say hi, I'm so & so's wife or husband or whatever. If there is infidelity going on and your significant other did not inform the other that he or she was married, then that small action will definitely introduce a new element to the playing field. Depending upon what type of individual the significant other is dealing with, the outcome could be anything from 'did you invite your husband or wife here to break up with me?' to 'this is my girl, who the hell are you and why are you kissing her?' In almost any relationship there will be lies. If it is a purely sexual relationship, there will be a lot of lies. From my experience, those who are involved with another on a purely sexual basis will eventually begin to have feelings for the other person, whether it be on the part of one or on the part of both and even if they continue to lie to each other and say it's only about the physical. The proof is in the proverbial pudding. If a sexual relationship is only about sex, then there will be no other feelings involved. There will be no getting upset if someone outside the extra marital relationship kisses the person who is cheating. There will be no concern if there is sexual contact or intercourse between that person and one or fifty others. It will or should be 'I'm here to have sex with you, then I'm going home and I don't care what you do after I leave or who you do it with.' But here's the problem - most people cannot separate the feelings that come along with a sexual relationship, no matter how much they lie about it. I have heard many people tell of how they were dealing with a married person on a sexual level and how they accepted the relationship between the husband and wife but refused to accept the very idea of the person they were sleeping with having sex with somebody else. I thought to myself, this is some real silly and hypocritical shit. How can a person in his or her right mind involve themselves in a relationship with a married man or woman but get upset when that married man or woman does the same thing? (…leads me to believe that people who cheat are not completely in their right minds…) For some this may get a tad bit confusing so I will use my hypothetical example people, Ryan, Tasha and Kim. Ryan and Kim are married. Ryan and Tasha are having an affair. Tasha is not completely fine with the fact that Ryan continues to sleep with Kim but reluctantly accepts the situation because they are married. Plus there is the recurring fact that Ryan continues to tell Tasha that he is soon going to leave Kim. Ryan starts sleeping with another woman and Tasha completely freaks out. Then Tasha wants to go and give Ryan hell for cheating on her. Do you understand why I say this is some silly shit? But this is the thinking process of many people in this world. I mentioned in my first book that infidelity is never simple and this is one of the reasons. This is the 'looking out for number one' mentality which contributes to making this world as messed up as it is. It is basically the same as someone saying 'I can jeopardize your peace of mind and stability but you can't do it to me.' You see some people with their twisted interpretations of love may actually feel that they are in fact in love, like Tasha in this hypothetical example. She could be deluding herself into thinking that Ryan loves her too and is just trying to keep the level of drama in his and Kim's relationship down by sleeping with aka pacifying her until she and him eventually break up. This type of thinking is silly also but more than that it is sad. It is sad because once Tasha realizes that Ryan is not going to leave her which is almost always the case, she will be heartbroken and possibly hell bent on revenge. People have to realize that infidelity is the same, whether it is with one or whether it is with one thousand. There is no moral dispute here, if you cheat, expect to be cheated on. I'm not saying it will happen that way but a person should put themselves into that mindset to avoid going crazy. When a person does this, understanding that whatever goes around, comes around, then the blow will not be as hard when or if and when this person who is cheating finds out that he or she is being cheated on as well. In my book, any committed relationship holds precedence over friends and casual acquaintances so there should be no problem if you see your husband or wife conversing with someone you haven't met and you walk right up and give your significant other a kiss. I may be alone here but I don't believe friends should be hidden. If you don't like your significant other's friends, that's one thing but you should at least know them. More importantly, they should know you.

There's another simple method used to catch cheaters – or if not catch them completely, at least put a little more doubt in the mind of a suspicious person. It's called the smell test. This method is self explanatory. All you need to do is smell your partner when they come home. In my first book, The Correct Way To Fool Around, I mentioned that cologne was something that people in relationships often pay attention to – especially when going to or coming from a night on the town. This can be a double edged sword because in many department stores as well as on certain streets, a person can at any time sample a multitude of different scents and as aggressive as many of the sales people in New York commonly are, it is not uncommon for one or two of them to spray some nasty scent on your hand without your permission. This is one of those many situations, which resemble infidelity. Think about it, if you are a somewhat suspicious person and your significant other comes home smelling like someone else or at least smelling of a scent, which is unfamiliar, wouldn't you be the least bit concerned? And on top of that, would you be the type of person to give them the benefit of the doubt or would you go straight into the accusatory phase? Anyway, getting back to smelling as a method of detecting infidelity, understand that there are several tactful ways to go about this. A person should not wait until their partner walks in the door, jump on them and start sniffing the way an anxious dog would but rather subtle, affectionate, closeness, beginning with a hug, then maybe some before shower foreplay. Reason for the before shower thing; a lot of men will fool around and scrub the lows but neglect the highs. In other words, if they are in a rush, they will wash their penis but not their armpits. Yes I agree not the most sanitary method of hygiene but some of these men; in an attempt to thwart their significant others' suspicions often assume the significant other will only smell that area. If a woman is suspicious and she has a particular smell in her mind (like that of another woman) and she smells a smell, which does not match the smell she anticipates, the thought of possible infidelity will be banished – at least for the time being. If however, the woman gives her man an all over subtle body sniff and one part, especially that part, smells different, there should and will be questions. What other possible reason can there be for smelling clean down there but not so clean everywhere else? With women, the air of doubt can be placed in their partner's mind if they come home smelling of cologne. This is where attention to detail really comes in because most women own at least a few bottles of perfume and many men don't pay attention to all of them but realizing that White Diamonds and Old Spice are not in any way closely related does not take a brain surgeon to figure out. Continuing with smells as a method of detection, it should be known that rubber has a very distinct smell. Latex condoms are made of rubber and the smell left on a person who has not washed properly after using one is not easily mistakable. People may try to use the excuse of exercise or sweat and often, exertion may produce a somewhat similar odor however the longer people are around each other, the more adept they become at distinguishing scents. What offers philanderers more and more opportunity is the fact that certain partners will group all the smells into one of two categories, good or bad. For instance a man may cheat with someone after he leaves work, then go workout at the gym for an hour or so, then head home to the significant other. The significant other, upon the man's arrival, may say something to the effect of 'hey honey, how was your day – you stink, go take a shower.' And the man will have an interior smile for the rest of the evening, because he knows he's gotten away with 'murder.' Now I am not suggesting for any man or woman to have intimate relations with a partner who smells less than desirable as a method of catching them in a lie or proving their unfaithfulness but something as simple as helping them undress before they take their shower will provide the close and unsuspecting type of contact, which may help to decipher a sweat smell from a condom smell. Believe it or not, there are some people who do not know what a condom smells like, be it due to those people only involving themselves in committed relationships after marriage, where the need was unnecessary or because they are in the type of relationship where sex is not yet an issue. For those innocent & suspecting people, purchase a pack of rubbers and get familiar with the scent. When I say get familiar with the scent, I'm not saying keep and compare whenever you have doubt, I'm saying (1) realize that all smells are not the same and (2) know exactly what it is you are looking for.

Vagueness

One of the things, which helps folks who are unsure about a partner's fidelity is the fact that guilty people are often vague with their answers when explaining their whereabouts. For instance, if questioned about a person's present location, they may say I'm in Manhattan instead of I'm on 86th street or they'll say 'I'm on my way home' or even 'I'm on my way to work.' Some people who are involved with these folks will just accept that answer and continue on with the next topic of conversation. Other people however, will pry and pry until they get a precise, military grid square location on your whereabouts and often will try to trick you by saying that they are at or close to that location themselves. In a case like that, a guilty person has but two options; one, get to the location they lied and said they were at before their partner does or two, inform their significant other that they are leaving that location for someplace closer to where they actually are. Vagueness has always been a very reliable indicator of guilt, deception or lack of education. What helps the guilty people is the fact that the innocents are not as diligent as they could be in trying to extract the desired information. Often what happens is the innocent party will ask 'where are you' to which the guilty or suspected party will reply 'I'm on the way home' or 'I'm on the way to somewhere' or 'I just left so and so's house' but mind you these people will answer your questions without divulging exactly where they presently are. 'I'm on the way to the job' could mean 'I just had sex with your sister and now I'm on the way to the job.' 'I just left so and so's house' could actually mean 'I just left so and so's house thirty minutes ago and I'm pulling into my boyfriend's driveway as we speak.' What the innocent people in relationships need to do is fully question the suspected significant other and not just until the significant other begins to get frustrated at the questioning but until you, the innocent party, are completely satisfied with all of the responses. There's one thing about guilty people, which I believe to be universal; they hate being questioned. If a person you are involved in a relationship with refuses to divulge specifics or gets mad behind the inquiry, that may not always mean he or she is cheating – BUT IT MIGHT! An innocent person should have very little to no reason at all to get upset behind his or her significant other wanting to know a few pieces of detailed information. Now if that desire to know turns into a full blown accusatory interrogation, then I can understand someone not wanting to answer. However if it's something like 'honey what street are you on' and the other says 'why' or hesitates in any shape, form or fashion, there's a possibility, however miniscule, that he or she may be doing something he or she does not want you to know about.

THE CORRECT WAY TO FOOL AROUND PART 2

If in a new relationship and unsure about the fidelity of a partner, there are several things a person can do to check. One of the easiest is distributing rope. Giving a person enough rope to hang themselves can be accomplished often by just watching and waiting for them to make mistakes. This particular method is instrumental in catching a person because the vast majority of people who are doing wrong won't necessarily take the proper precautions to cover their tracks unless they have reason to believe someone is watching. First off, if possible, don't let them know you have caller id. If they know you do, tell them it's broken. Using the caller ID, document each and every call you receive from your significant other. Ask them to state their exact location at each call. Don't do it verbatim, as in what's your exact location? Ask something like, 'hey honey, where are you now?' Ask a question, which does not sound too much like you're prying but make it direct enough that it can only warrant one type of answer - the one you want. If they call you from 673 - 0000 and say it's the payphone on the corner of Main Street & Halibut Avenue and then call sometime later from the same number and say it's their cousin's house, then you've caught them in a lie. Remember all cheaters lie and lies are usually the first step in catching a cheater. Now before any of you reading this run out and file divorce papers because the above scenario has happened to you, I must inform you that technology changes every day. In regard to the example above about the phone number showing up on the caller id, there are new phones recently introduced to the market which have the capability to trick another's caller id – and by this I mean a person can call another and have almost any number show up on the caller id as the number or location the person is calling from. There is also an ingenious invention that is available for purchase at certain retailers called the spoof card, which basically does the same thing. The benefit of these measures is that the person you are trying to catch in an indiscretion may already know you suspect him or her and may use these instruments to throw you off your plan of capturing them. Think about it, if you're at work and you suspect your wife of cheating - and you call the house and she doesn't pick up the phone – and then you call her cell phone and she responds, and you ask her why she didn't pick up the house phone, she can say anything to the effect of 'something's wrong with the house phone.' What she can then do to further her story is call you back using one of the above methods, making the house number appear on your caller id, leading you to believe that maybe there's actually something wrong with the incoming service.

This next method of detection is not new – it is the method, which has gotten petty criminals, sexual predators and even store cashiers caught during their transgressions for years. It is the hidden video camera. People, as smart as they are – as technologically advanced as they are, still make stupid mistakes. One of those stupid mistakes is assuming that because something is not seen, then there is nothing to be seen. People don't realize that there are many kinds of covert cameras, which are much smaller than one inch in diameter. Think for a second what could be done with a camera or recording device that small. Technology that tiny allows, rather forces a person to be themselves, meaning that since they think no one is watching or listening, they can bring over someone of the opposite sex while the husband or wife is at work or maybe they can masturbate on the kitchen counter or maybe even divulge secret same sex fantasies to another person whom they trust. People know that there is an expectation of certain behavior in society that most civilized and respectable individuals must adhere to. This behavior is not always the behavior that these people would exude if they were home alone or if they knew for certain they were not in the public eye. You have to sometimes ask yourself, why is it when there are big, bulky, noticeable cameras at a workplace or bank for instance, there are few to no instances of horseplay or debauchery - yet when there are no cameras or recording devices, these institutions have higher instances of thefts and lawsuits. It's because when people see opportunity, nine times out of ten, they will seize it. Cameras such as these – called spy cams are not as expensive as most may think. They can be purchased at spy or counter spy retailers or at many camera shops and often they can be installed without professional assistance. I installed a few of these spy cams in my home and not to make kinky sex movies – even though I heard they are great for that – but just to see what I could see and to my surprise, I got more than an eyeful. Aside from what was mentioned above about a young lady sneaking another dude into my house, there was an instance of my girlfriend at the time counting a fistful of money – and no, I'm not talking about ones, I'm talking about the type of money which has zeros on it. I mentioned to her that something family related had come up and asked her later that evening if she had any money and guess what she said – no, I'm broke, could I borrow some from you. Ain't that some shit? The bottom line here is that cameras are an essential part of eradicating the thought of infidelity in the home or office or wherever you may have doubt. They take away the mystery and wonder of not knowing, which can cause a person to literally lose his or her mind. It should be known though that if you have to resort to actually spying on a significant other without his or her knowledge, then your relationship is pretty much gone. I don't want to hear any of that nonsense about 'I just wanna be sure he or she is a good person' because everybody reading this book knows as well as I that whenever a person has to spy on another to make sure that person is not doing anything wrong, there is no longer trust in that relationship. The only time I believe it is okay to spy on anyone in a relationship is when that relationship is between a parent and a young child. Children do not get into relationships. Again, if the need arises for spying – you're either dating a child, you're a child yourself or there is no trust in the relationship.

Often a person who is involved in an affair may use the maze of employment to hide his or her transgressions. The employment excuse works so well and is called a maze because many people nowadays work in high rise buildings or in offices, which have more than one floor and many different telephone extensions. All a person who is cheating would have to do is inform his significant other that he will be working on several different floors on a particular day or working on a different floor than what he or she is accustomed to and then for backup, inform someone who has access to his phone, to say that he has just left, should anyone happen to call. What a multitude of cheaters do or should I say do not do is give the person they're cheating on any type of credit for having common sense. These cheaters are often so preoccupied with their transgressions that they forget or neglect to think that maybe the ones they're cheating on already have reason to suspect them. People are so used to being corrected if and when they do something wrong that if they aren't, they are often disillusioned into thinking that they have succeeded in their wrongdoing. They think that because a mate does not say anything regarding a person's actions, nothing is wrong. What these people don't realize is that this world is built on sneakiness. In the military, one of the most basic lessons taught for success in combat is the element of surprise. Law enforcement does not walk up to a suspected criminal's front door and arrest them without evidence or a warrant as much as they will stake out the same and wait until that person makes the desired mistake. (Most times anyway.) Law enforcement does not come a knocking at four in the afternoon looking for those who may have fractured a law or two either. They come by at six in the damn morning when most people with common sense who if not working are asleep. The reason this tactic is so successful is because few people expect to be woken up at that ungodly hour – especially for the purpose of getting dressed, handcuffed and escorted through the lobby of their building where all the nosey neighbors who are on their way to work can get a birds eye view of ya. Anyway when it comes to detecting infidelity, the innocent parties in a relationship always have the upper hand and this is mainly because cheaters too often forget. Cheaters lie and not only do they lie, they have to remember the lie or lies they told. Innocent people are much more proficient at remembering stories which were told to them – so consequently they will be much better at remembering the lies the cheater told – even if the cheater doesn't. Continuing with the phone calls from above, a cheater may call you from ten different numbers and just because they feel they have to stay one step ahead or because they are trying to remember too many things at one time, may lie about their locations, when on the phone. Jot down each and every number they call from and at which time they call. Make a new icon on your desktop, which says questionable calls or just maintain that log in a secret place. Later you can make comparisons but in the meantime, keep this record so that if they call again and say something to contradict what they've said before, you've caught them in a lie - and like I've previously mentioned, catching someone in a lie, especially a lie about the opposite sex, is the first step in catching a cheater.

This next method is not recommended for everyone. It is recommended for those who had had to deal with prior bouts of infidelity or repeated bouts of unproven accusations. Since many cheaters will often subconsciously project their guilt onto the innocent party, a good idea may be to check the activities of the suspected party; more specifically the phone messages. Some people who are cheating will go through great lengths to cover their indiscretions, like putting lock codes on their cell phones and such. This in itself should be concentrated on because in a trusting relationship what need would there be for doing this? But there are others in relationships who believe that there is an ample amount of trust in the relationship - so much so that they may become lax in hiding their transgressions altogether. Some of these people who are cheating do not consider the cheating as such. They consider the fact that they are sleeping with a married man or woman nothing more than a wrinkle in the fabric of their otherwise perfect relationship. They will act like the relationship is just between them and the person who is married. They will call and ask the person they are sleeping with to come over and bring certain items like food or household supplies, the same way a husband or wife would. If the person involved in the affair does not answer the phone be it for whatever reason, the other will often leave the above message or something to that effect. Now ask yourself, if you were to check your husband's phone and you heard a message from some other woman who is not a relative to the effect of 'bring some Chinese food when you get in' or 'can you buy me this?' wouldn't you be the least bit concerned? Of course you would. There is an invisible line that people in relationships and those outside of relationships should not cross. Asking a married man or woman for certain things without the significant other's knowledge is not conducive to a happy relationship. It will cause doubt in any relationship because the first thing the wife of the man in this hypothetical example above will say is 'why is she asking you, a married man to do her bidding?' Now even if there is nothing derogatory going on, the fact that the question was asked will cause problems. This and things like this is what people need to be on the lookout for. Checking for messages such as these will not provide absolute proof but they will provide much insight into if not what's going on in the life of the significant other, then what type of acquaintances the significant other has. Now I know there are at least a thousand people waiting to say if you trust your partner you shouldn't be looking through their stuff or if you look for stuff, you're gonna find stuff. And these people may be right in their own respects but 1) if a relationship is open and honest, meaning there is ongoing communication, there would most likely not be any factors which would drive someone to undertake the above mentioned methods. But this is one of the problems in relationships; people don't talk to each other, and when people in relationships are not indulging in conversation, the belief often is that somebody is hiding something - hence the employment of the above method. 2) If there was nothing going on to begin with and a person went through the other's property, phone for instance, there would be nothing to hide and consequently no, rather little reason to get mad and 3) this is how trust is manipulated. A conniving person will say 'I trust you, I don't go through your things so why should you have the need or desire to go through mine?' and then the other person will say something soft like 'yea I guess you're right, I'm sorry.' Then they will give up the pursuit of information - and the other who is probably cheating will say 'phew, I dodged a bullet!' I tell people this all the time, love and trust never enter a relationship at exactly the same time, they never leave a relationship at exactly the same time and they are almost never at the same intensity as with the other party during the union.

Cheating is a conscious decision usually made by consenting adults of legal age. Whenever not, that is when the criminal aspect comes in. What is usually agreed upon when infidelity is present is the 'yea, I'm married but I'm going to screw this other woman' or the 'yea I'm married but I'm going to let this other guy screw me.' This decision is not forced, it is basically an action, which precedes another action. To catch someone in the act of infidelity, a conscious decision to be diligent in performing certain measures must be made also. Now what I often suggest to people who ask me how to catch someone they suspect of infidelity is to hire a private investigator. Many people are cheap or if not cheap, feel that their friends can do the job just as easily. The difference I have seen between private investigators and friends is that with private investigators, its business – with friends it's often personal. People will give someone they know, someone who is a friend $50 or $100 to follow their husband or wife and report back any derogatory information. The problem with this is that most times when the above technique is employed the friends who are hired are not as competent as private investigators who have been trained. These untrained people will often let emotions dictate their actions, meaning if a man sees his best friend's wife talking to another fellow who neither of the two men know, he may be prompted to tell the husband more than what actually occurred – to wit; instead of 'I saw your wife talking to a gentleman yesterday' the report could resemble 'I saw your wife hanging out with some dude.' Instead of a husband meeting a female co-worker or even driving that co-worker to the office, the report again could resemble something to the effect of 'I saw your man driving this bitch around town.' Notice the difference in the two. People have to be objective in their observations and this is one of the things private investigators are trained to do. They will not say 'yeah girl, he cheating on you' just because a married man gives a woman a hug and a kiss on the cheek. They will report just the facts as they happen and let you form your conclusions on your own, the way it should be. The reason many people shy away from using them is because they are not cheap. A good investigator can easily run you over $100 an hour. They are recommended because the information you desire will more than likely be the information you receive and it will more than likely be based on actual fact rather than speculation. Far too often people speculate on the activities going on in their relationships – and even more often do they end those relationships based on the result of that speculation. It should be noted that speculation is <u>never</u> a proper method to use when deciphering whether or not infidelity is present in your relationship because speculation is <u>nothing more than a conclusion based on incomplete information or evidence.</u> So if you find a condom in your husband's car, it doesn't automatically mean he is, has been or was just about to cheat. It means that there is a situation present which needs explaining. If you find pictures in your wife's phone of some dude naked, it does not mean she is, has been or is about to cheat. It means that there is a situation present which again, needs explaining. Now I know there is someone out there saying oh hell no! This is pure, clear cut infidelity! For this person and others like him or her I will explain the two examples from my personal experience. Once after work, I gave several coworkers a ride to their homes simply because I had a car and they didn't. They lived close to my neighborhood so I figured what harm could it do? One of those coworkers had a condom on his person which I later found out dropped from his pocket and onto the floor of my vehicle. Now I don't know if it was his intent to drop the condom there just to see what would happen (I have acquaintances who do things like that just for kicks) or what but imagine my surprise when the lady I was involved with at the time burst into the house reciting that question no man ever wants to hear. 'What the fuck is this doing in your car?' Now all I could say was the absolute truth and that was 'I don't know - probably belongs to somebody who was in my car.' What comes next? The follow up interrogation questions: 'who was in your car?' 'Why did they have the need for condoms?' And the biggie, 'were you planning on using this condom with this person you had in your car?' This is not infidelity but a situation which resembles such. There is no easy way out of this unless the complete truth is told (which it was) and trust from the other party prevails. (which it didn't). It was pretty much downhill from there relationship wise but that incident did teach me a valuable lesson; if there isn't trust in the beginning of a relationship, there very possibly may never be. Oh and always check the car if you deal with somebody who has severe issues with trust. As for finding pictures of some random naked dude in my significant others phone, I found out after the fact that the photos were taken by a so called friend of my significant other. My significant other at the time and I lived apart from one another and she had lent her apartment to the woman to carry on her indiscretion behind her husbands back. For some reason or other, she wanted to have a record of her conquests I guess and used my girlfriend's camera phone to take the pictures. Now I don't know if her intent was to let me find the pictures and subsequently break up behind that or not but that's what happened. We did get back together after the truth came out but the reason we broke up temporarily was because the trust was not there. Combine that with the fact that almost all of my girlfriend's friend's were garden tools aka hoes - it made it that much more easy to believe that she was just as bad. You might as well call it a learning experience because she and I eventually broke up for other trust related issues and she and the so called friend of hers parted ways as well. Like I mentioned before, if there is no trust in a relationship, there is nothing! One final note; even though these were proven to be examples of things which resemble infidelity, that does not mean that if there were to happen in your world, the same result would apply. A person who finds a condom in the significant other's car could have evidence of infidelity. A person who finds pictures of somebody naked in the significant others camera phone could have evidence of infidelity as well. Unless you have absolute proof or an admission, then evidence like what was found above is pretty much circumstantial. Try to catch them with their pants down. That way they can't dispute shit!

Some people who play part time private eye often think they have evidence of a partner's infidelity but they should be warned, the mind plays tricks – especially when in collusion with the heart. There are many people out here who think they know things they don't actually know – and they will often use their dimwitted logic to make another's life a living hell. One of the most consistent indicators of this has been the 'I know what a cell phone sounds like when its turned off.' What people who are suspicious of their partners will do is call their home or job and if they are unable to get in contact, will then call that person's cell phone. Some of these geniuses will automatically interpret the call immediately going to voicemail as the cell phone being turned off. Now it's very possible that the person who is being called is a low life who is cheating and just happens to have his or her phone turned off at the time but that does not hold true for everybody. It's also very possible that the network could be busy or could be having technical difficulties. It's also possible that another call could be coming in at exactly the same time. Some people are so stubborn and unwilling to listen to a possible explanation that they think anytime a cell phone call goes directly to voicemail, the only acceptable reason is because the phone is turned off. These geniuses also don't bother to think that there are hundreds upon hundreds of cell phone companies as well as hundreds upon hundreds of different types of cell phones. Each one does not work the same. Let me say that again, each one does not work the same. I know of several people who have broken up because of what was not truth but what they wanted to believe was truth and when people have a negative or wrong thought in their mind, which they believe in wholeheartedly, almost nothing in this world will change that. Granted, there are dropped calls from cell phones all the time. There are also dead zones, which we as normal human beings do not have the capability to know when we are working in or walking through one. Some of the messages that many of these cell phone companies are so delighted to leave get people in trouble also. One of those messages is 'the person you have called has traveled outside the calling area.' Note: this message is not always true. Many times this is nothing more than a pre recorded message companies use to make themselves as well as the person receiving the call seem more important than he or she actually is. The problem with this is that the significant other of the individual with this type of answering machine is many times insecure, jealous and whatever else and will after hearing this message, jump to all types of conclusions, the least being 'your message said you were traveling outside of the calling area today...so where were you?' Just like with computers, there is <u>always</u> the possibility of technical failure such as crashing but some people just don't want to accept that. Some disillusioned people in this world think that things never go awry. They think that cars never break down or trains and buses always run on schedule or that technology is infallible. Again, once people have in their mind a particular belief, such as a person is cheating or they are doing or have done something foul, there is little anyone can do to dispel those beliefs. There is a very popular talk show whose host, I think keeps beating the hell out of the proverbial dead horse. The majority of this particular show's topics revolve around two things, one; denial of paternity – more specifically 'I'm 100% sure I'm not the baby's father!' or 'I know you've been cheating and I'm here today to prove it!' The tests used on the show from my understanding, are generally DNA and polygraphs. DNA you cannot dispute due to the fact that it is extremely unlikely that any two unrelated individuals possess identical DNA, and because of the fact that a child's DNA will always share some of the same characteristics as the DNA of his or her parent. Polygraphs you can dispute because they generally only record changes, which occur in reaction to questions. Some of the changes, which are measured, are blood pressure, pulse rate and perspiration. This is disputable because nervousness, as well as other factors, can affect perspiration and pulse rate and maybe even blood pressure. Many of these relationships on the show are ended because people want to believe a machine instead of their partner. I'm not saying the machine is always right or wrong but if a person in a relationship is willing to choose science over their relationship, then the relationship was over long before they got to the show. One of them just wanted somebody or something else to be on their side.

There is a great amount of spying & counter spying in this

country, done by several high profile & hush hush agencies. These agencies use the latest technology and believe it or not, some of this technology is available to the general public. Tracking devices, hidden cameras and even phone taps are for sale at many spy stores or counter spy stores and are not as expensive as most may think. Employing the use of these and other devices is becoming increasingly more popular because of terrorism, infidelity, corporate espionage and lastly because of the overwhelming need to know. There are many people in this world who suffer from the overwhelming need to know. These people have hidden cameras in their homes, listening and recording devices attached to their phones and computers. If you are on the side of the people who want to know, then the spy store is the place for you. If you are on the side of the people who cheat, you have but only a few options: keep your mouth shut while at home, take your natural partner way, way, far away from anybody either of you may know or check out the counter spy store for methods to foil the significant other who is trying to foil you.

In conclusion, it must be stated that the only true detector of a person's fidelity is complete and unarguable evidence. Not the heart, not the conscience, not speculation and definitely not evidence, which is purely circumstantial. Now while there are many feelings, which can let you know when something is not right in the relationship, the feelings, which signify the opposite are often misleading. People by nature want to believe their relationship is doing well. They want to give the benefit of the doubt to the other party. Unfortunately this desire for happiness can often put aside common sense, which will let a person know all things are not as they seem. If you suspect your partner of cheating but don't see it or your partner suspects you and doesn't see it, it didn't happen. Trust me, you will drive yourself crazy trying to prove it. Even the most inept, disorganized, klutz has at least a basic level of smarts, when it comes to hiding something from someone else, especially when they know that that something will get him or her in trouble. The best and simplest advice when trying to detect someone's fidelity or lack of is time. Time is one of the most powerful resources we have when it comes to finding things out. Time heals old wounds. Time empowers the conscience. <u>Time extracts truth.</u> The one thing about time is the fact that it is not a friend of a person's memory. The longer the period of time passes in a relationship, the longer a person, rather a person who has committed infidelity has to forget the actual truth or the lie that person told to the significant other. Just wait and watch. Everything done in the dark will eventually come to light.

Chapter Seven
Secrets; The Building Blocks To Failure

Possessing a secret, something that no one else knows, is a form of power. It is a form of power, which extends from one end of the spectrum to the other. A secret can send a person into a deep depression, as in knowing they have only months to live. On the other hand a secret can be extremely uplifting, as in you being the only who knows you hold the winning ticket to a multi million dollar lottery. Secrets can be a blackmail tool or a bargaining chip. For instance, if an employee knows the boss is cheating, that employee can threaten to tell the bosses' significant other in exchange for guaranteed stability or for a better position at the job. Secrets can give a person peace of mind because depending upon how damaging, a person can hold that secret over somebody's head indefinitely. Secrets are good and bad, except in relationships. When two people make a commitment to each other, often they pledge fidelity, trust and honesty. Secrecy, if not a direct violation of the previous three, will make someone in a relationship believe it is a direct violation of at least one of those three and many times the belief is worse than the actual indiscretion. After a certain amount of time in a relationship, one person's actions often become a direct result of the other's, as in if you do something to me I'll do something to you. There is also the barter system belief of if you do for me I'll do for you. This sometimes stems from the basic childhood teachings of if somebody hits you; you hit him or her back. When one party is keeping secrets and the other party finds out about it, whether they know the secret or not, that party will either attempt to uncover the secret or begin keeping secrets of his or her own. If one of the people in the relationship believes the other is being unfaithful, that person will continue to believe that as long as the other does nothing to dispel those beliefs. What's worse is that as long as that type of insecurity exists, a person will act on those beliefs – up to and including cheating. Insecurity should be considered secrecy's worst enemy because when one partner is insecure and the other partner is keeping secrets, the only thing left is distrust. When there's distrust in a relationship, the end of the relationship is usually not far away. I believe everybody in this world has at least one thing they want no one else or very few others to find out about and it doesn't necessarily have to be murder or anything of that magnitude but I do not believe anybody's life should be an open book either. The level of secrecy, combined with the level of security or insecurity of a person's significant other is what will damage a relationship. Talking about past relationships can be helpful in finding out or understanding why certain problems exist in the present relationship but hiding the past relationships especially when they affect the present one is a recipe for disaster. Keeping in contact with an ex can be looked at from both the good and the bad end of the spectrum. If there were children involved, then staying in not so close contact can be a good thing, as long as both parties in the present relationship understand and accept that type of relationship. If, on the other hand however the past relationship was purely a physical one, then keeping in contact will certainly bring about the memories of that physical relationship and may even bring about the 'let's do it one more time for old times sake.' Plus, keeping in contact with an ex that your partner knows about will cause severe problems if your ex doesn't know about your partner. That type of contact will lead to suspicion or should I say 'extreme suspicion' as to why you won't tell the past about the present. Secrets are generally viewed as bad because there is almost always a dark connotation associated with them. The first thing a person thinks of when the word secret is uttered is it must be something derogatory – or at least 'juicy.' The general consensus is 'if it's not bad, why then is it a secret?' If secrets weren't bad or juicy, people would just consider them regular, old, run of the mill gossip. Secrets have no place in a happy and productive relationship, which usually embraces positive and ongoing communication. The only places I can actually see a secret being a positive thing is if it relates to a surprise party or event or if it is instrumental in preventing harm to someone.

Secrets will cause, at the very least, perturbation in a relationship especially if one partner is under the illusion that there is total honesty between the two. Total honesty is extremely rare, if not non existent in relationships. Total honesty means never having a secret to keep. Total honesty is the same as complete trust, something many people disillusion themselves into believing they have or are capable of achieving. This comes about from people believing they or their partners are above doing wrong. They feel that since I would never do that to you, you should never have reason to do it to me and if one person keeps a secret, which the other finds out about, that person's feeling of betrayal can stretch as far as that person's mind will allow it to go. Total honesty means being brutally honest, where you may often have to hurt a person's feeling's to avoid any type of misunderstanding. In my opinion, it's best not to keep secrets at all but this will never happen because in a relationship there will always be things a person will not want their partner to know and as history has shown, the less hurtful the secret the better. There must be a balance. This is where communication or the lack of can help or end the relationship. If a couple discusses the problems that the secrets are causing, meaning getting them out in the open, they have a much better chance at rectifying whatever problems the secrets are causing. If a couple ignores the problem, chances are the secrets will eventually be one of the causes of the couple's inevitable breakup and not because of the actual secret but because of the fact that a secret was being kept. A person does not need to know what the secret was for it to destroy his or her relationship. Secrets will make a person's mind wonder and the bad part about that is that a person's mind has infinite wondering capabilities. This basically means that if a person you are involved with has a secret that you know of or has a secret that you only know part of and they refuse to divulge the rest of the information to you, depending on your level of insecurity, that secret can blossom into the worst conspiracy theory imaginable. There are many types of secrets couples in relationships keep from one another. The reasons these secrets are kept can vary from fear of losing one's partner to fear of losing one's life. Just like reasons for cheating, there is no set number for the amount of secrets, which can destroy a relationship. The only definite thing about them, just like cheating reasons is that they will always vary in intensity. Some are teency, weency and some are damaging beyond belief. The most popular secrets I have noticed in relationships are health, sex, personal, relationship and financial and the content of each one of these secrets can extend from one end of the spectrum to the other. Here's an example of the most popular secrets couples keep from one another:

Health – 'I have an incurable sexually transmitted disease.' 'I have a curable sexually transmitted disease.' 'I have a terminal illness, which has nothing to do with sex.'

Sexual – 'I was born one gender but had a sex change before you met me. I'm gay or bisexual. I told you I only had sex with one other person in my life but it was more like forty.' 'I'm addicted to sex.'

Personal – 'I'm not the person you believe me to be. Remember the person you saw on America's Most Wanted who you said looks like me and I told you it was coincidence, well it was a bigger coincidence than you thought.'

Relationship – 'I'm still involved in a physical relationship with my children's parent.' 'I really hate relationships.' 'I have never had a relationship last more than a month.' 'I really don't like you but I will have sex with you because you have a gorgeous body.'

Financial – 'I told you I was broke and unemployed but I have a trust fund worth seventy eight million. I didn't tell you initially because I wanted to make sure you loved me for me.'

As I mentioned before, there are good and bad secrets but those, which would have had an adverse effect on a relationship, like the first four, have no place in a relationship. Secrets, which would determine whether a person gets involved with another or not had that person known ahead of time are not the types of things relationships should be based on. The last example about a person withholding financial information is understandable and not such a bad thing, especially when you consider the level of greed and deception in this world. If you are financially secure and are dealing with someone who is not or will probably never be, then it might not be such a bad idea to make sure that the person you are planning to involve yourself with is willing to give his or her all for you. People will play whatever role necessary to achieve what their hearts and wallets desire. It's rare to find any person in this world who would love another who has nothing material to offer but I believe the person who would is truly in love. One of the most detrimental things about secrets is that they make many people in relationships too afraid to be themselves. These people often fit themselves into a 'whatever my significant other likes is what I am' shell and they do this all to avoid the dreaded confrontation over feelings. In a happy relationship, a couple will usually do what causes the least amount of disturbed feelings for each other. If a man is doing something the woman doesn't like, more often than not, she will in one way or another inform him. The man will inform his partner also, maybe in a totally different way but he will inform her as well. Many people nowadays place their happiness above all else. If someone is not catering to their feelings, in other words making them happy, they will leave in search of someone who can. These people in relationships often don't want to lose what they have and will not risk giving the ultimatum 'this is me take it or leave it' because chances are the other will choose the less desired option. True, this is how many fake relationships get started but what needs to be addressed is not the fact that the secret itself was kept but why. Some people will perpetrate this kind of trickery because they want sexual favors and nothing else. There, in my opinion is no excuse for this type of behavior. Let a person know where your true intentions lie. If they accept you, great, if not, move on. There will be thousands upon thousands of others willing to indulge you in a 'friends with benefits' type of relationship. Trust me. Some others will perpetrate this kind of trickery because they know the person they are involved with is a 'good' catch but they themselves are not exactly what the 'good' catch is looking for. The person who is not what the 'good' catch is looking for will do **whatever** it takes to keep the other happy. This would be a very noble form of trickery if the act of trickery contained any type of nobility but the major problem with this is that sooner or later, a person's true colors will always spill out. And when they do, that's usually about the time the significant other who has believed that the false you was actually the real you will say something to the effect of 'you've changed!' Here's an example: as friends, a man and a woman can walk down the street and talk about anybody and be as explicitly verbal as possible. That man can tell his opposite sex friend that some woman, whom they both observe, has a nice physique. A woman who has a completely platonic male friend (who is not gay) can mention to him that another man tickles her fancy and there should be no problem. When people get together however, they often restrict their conversation and behavior because (1) they think they always know how their partners will respond and (2) because they are afraid of crossing any invisible parameters, set by their partners, which will be interpreted as disrespect. Let's look at the above examples using people who have been in a not completely trusting relationship. The man: 'I think she has a nice shape.' The woman: 'So what does that mean, you wanna fuck her or something?' Some people in relationships progress in such a way, which causes them to interpret and analyze everything, which is said instead of just accepting. This type of progression causes each partner to search for things or clues, which may signal an impending breakup. Second scenario – The woman: 'I think that guy is very attractive.' The man: So you don't think I'm attractive anymore?' Many people in relationships expect their partners to have tunnel vision when it comes to other people especially those of the opposite sex. People become so engrossed in one another that the slightest deviation is often interpreted as interest instead of observation. Ever notice how men act one way when they are around their male friends and act totally different around their girlfriends & wives? Women are guilty of this behavior too. People do this because they are keeping secrets. They are being themselves around their friends but are being the ones their significant others want them to be when they are around them. The difference in 'personalities' is basically the outlet the 'perpetrators' need to keep their sanity. If a person is forced to live a way, which is contradictory to their actual selves, they will be miserable after a period of time. Some people choose to live a double life and this is not as stressful as the ones who are forced but eventually both types of people will be unhappy. It's a revolving cycle – act one way to get the person I want. Act another way to keep the friends I've got. Just as long as the acting sessions don't overlap, meaning the friends don't see the husband acting like Mr. Mom and the wife doesn't see the husband acting like a hood on the street corner, drinking and gawking at other women, everything will be fine. Many times people are correct in the two above assumptions because the more time a couple spends together, the more they get to know and understand how each other will react to certain impulses and provocations. Knowing a certain level of a partner's potential reactions is good but what this level of knowledge also does is scare people into the mindset of 'I cannot be myself because my partner will not completely like me if I do.' Some men cannot talk to their women about other women because they believe their women will feel that conversation is always stemming from or leading to something sexual as opposed to a general observation. Some women cannot talk to their men because they feel their men won't understand them as a friend of the same sex would. This creates tension and apprehension in relationships, which are, if not destined for failure, at least headed for unhappiness.

Chapter Eight
Triggers

When it comes to infidelity, if a person catches their partner in an affair, whether they forgive that person or not, there will always be triggers. Triggers are things, which set off other things – such as an action or series of events. A trigger on a gun, when depressed, will set off a big bang. A trigger, when relating to memories in a relationship, will set off a bang of a different kind. For instance, if a person in a relationship gets cheated on by someone with red hair then later on down the line, they see someone else with red hair who maybe just remotely reminds them of the person who cheated, chances are exceptionally well they will be reminded of the indiscretion. If a person is married and their significant other takes a job in a place where only the opposite sex works and an affair happens, the strength of the relationship will of course be tested. If the couple decides to stay together and the cheating partner leaves that job but eventually takes another in a place occupied only by the opposite sex, whether the innocent partner is insecure or not, the fact that the same circumstances exist will trigger the memory. Here's another example.

My sister cheated with my ex boyfriend. I forgave her but now I have a new boyfriend and I'm hesitant about taking him around her. Is it wrong that I can't get the first situation out of my head, is it because I don't really forgive her or is it that every time I think about my sister or every time I think about somebody having an affair, what my sister and my ex did clouds my mind? Infidelity is one of the few things, which almost anything else will trigger the memory of. If a person's significant other was involved in an affair on a bright, sunny day in August, any bright, sunny day could possibly trigger or bring about the memory. If an affair was initiated due to an argument, the next argument, whether it be the same or the following relationship will most likely stir up the memory of the affair. There is no statute of limitations on triggers. Something derogatory can happen to a person during his teenage years and can be forgotten or placed in the back of his mind for twenty, thirty maybe even forty years down the road. All it will take however is for one word or one TV scene or one trip back to where the actual event took place, to send a person rushing back down memory lane. When a person cheats and gets caught, constantly being reminded of the transgression is one of the worst punishments. That, in a very small way, can be looked at as someone who while intoxicated commits vehicular manslaughter, where a completely innocent child is the victim and the person responsible beats the charge but has to drive to work everyday down the street were the accident took place. Being the innocent party in an infidelity situation is mentally punishing and having the ability to forgive but not forget is a punishment as well because just like the accident example, the innocent party will have to relive the indiscretion again and again. Innocent people in infidelity situations get hurt many times over; first when the actual act of infidelity occurs, then again each time they are reminded. Reminders or triggers come in all shapes and sizes. For instance, a person in a relationship could've had an affair with someone who drives a blue Nissan Maxima and have gotten caught. Even though months or years may go by its very possible that each time a blue Nissan Maxima happens to drive by, a reminder will pop into that innocent person's head encouraging them to think about their partner's affair. The good thing about these reminders or triggers is that eventually they will begin to fade. The bad thing about them is no matter how much time goes by, they will never completely disappear. It's been said that time heals all wounds. Unfortunately as history has repeatedly proven, time can only alleviate the memories of infidelity, not eradicate them. Triggers all too often remind us of the negative things we had to endure during our lives but they also have the capability to wreak havoc on our guilty consciences by reminding us of what we have done to other people. Let's say you cheated on someone and did not get away with the transgression. There will be more than a sufficient amount of 'triggers' to remind you of your wrongdoing, least of which, having the person you cheated on and every member of their family threatening to do you bodily harm. Now let's say you cheated with someone and you were fortunate enough not to get caught but the person you cheated on had suspicions, which although not able to be proven, caused a level of hurt in that person, that was not easily matched or forgotten. Watching that person cry because they felt you were cheating but were unsure, at the time made you laugh but now makes you feel an unsettling amount of guilt and every time you see someone hurt because of unproven accusations regarding infidelity, it hurts you. Every time you hear of someone getting away with cheating, it triggers a feeling of hurt, which is equal to what you caused this one particular person. Not a good feeling is it? Triggers affect a person from both sides, the side of the victim as well as that of the perpetrator – and just like from the side of the victim, the triggers affecting the perp side will lessen over time but will never completely go away.

Chapter Nine
Can Trust Ever Really Be Rebuilt?

In my first book, The Correct Way To Fool Around, I had suggested rebuilding trust as an effective means of recovering from infidelity. Since then I have been inundated with calls and emails from everybody who has been involved in a relationship, which has unfortunately been tainted by an affair. It seems that some people took my words out of context. I meant that rebuilding trust was an effective <u>start</u> for recovering from infidelity; I did not say however that that was all which was necessary for a successful relationship nor did I imply that everyone was completely adept at doing it. Some of these people who disputed my advice believe that once a couple's fidelity is marred by an affair, there is little or no chance at reconciliation. Some of these people, instead of trying to rebuild trust after an affair, will break it down even further. They will accuse their partner at every possible opportunity, never give them the benefit of the doubt or in short, never forgive them for the affair and they will do this, just as a way of punishing them for committing the original transgression. Many of these people are unhappy but stay in these types of relationships because they don't feel like 'starting over.' They don't particularly desire to relive the feelings of insecurity, the getting to know each other arguments or the holding in of farts and other bodily functions so that their potential mate will think they are perfect. Some people get comfortable in this manner to the point of being complacent. When in a relationship, people have a certain level of knowledge about the person they are involved with.

The longer people stay in a relationship, usually the greater that level of knowledge becomes. Whether these people are happy with their partners or not, at least they are aware of what they do and do not like. The ratio could be ten to one – ten being the things one person doesn't like and one being the thing that person does but at least they know. To stop an unhappy relationship after so long and start anew, a person would have to go back to square one to find out what they do or do not like in somebody else and what they have in common. Many people don't have the time or patience or vulnerability to do that. If relationships were to resemble certain educational institutions, where one could transfer partner history like they can credits, people would never be single.

Can trust ever really be rebuilt is one of those questions, which ranks right up there with the ever so philosophical, what am I doing here? This is a question, which has no right or wrong answer but more an answer, which is catered to the specific opinions of an individual. As with the 'what am I doing here' inquiry, everybody is here for a specific purpose or vocation. As with the rebuilding trust, everybody has his or her own methods and techniques, as well as time limits on recovery. Couples do not always break up at the same time nor do they always make up that way. When I say breakup, I don't mean the actual parting, I mean reaching the point of unhappiness, which leads up to the separation. One person in an unhappy relationship is almost always unhappier than the other and that one person almost always wants to breakup completely, while the other usually wants to try and work it out. When couples who are separated attempt to get back together, there is almost always an uneven momentum, meaning although both may desire reconciliation, one may try a little harder than the other to reach that goal. In regards to rebuilding, one couple can be willing to start trusting a week after an indiscretion is uncovered whereas another couple may not be willing to lower its defenses towards each other for a year. The amount of trust a person has within is not the same as the amount of trust held by anyone else. Trust is dependent upon several things, for example, how long a person is known, how trustworthy they make themselves seem to others and how willing a person is to let themselves be put in a position of vulnerability, to name a few. Trust is allowing one's self to be completely open with another person. In short, trust is basically the equivalent of putting all of your eggs in one basket. One of the more disheartening things I heard, which was consistent in almost all of the calls and emails I'd received was the belief that once a person cheats, that person will always cheat. Some people are completely unforgiving in this area. As I stated above, some people feel that cheating is the one thing to which there is no redemption. I find however that the previous statement is not as true as people make it out to be. Sure, there are going to be people in relationships who are going to cheat and quite a few of those people are going to get caught but all of those people are not going to be instant and lifelong criminals of passion because of that one transgression. The big misconception held by a few misguided and hurt souls is if a person hurts you, they should be made to perform some kind of penance or community service until the day they die. If a person cheats on another and gets caught, true, there should be some kind of retribution, just not the overwhelming, mental anguish backlash that many people see fit. Granted, if a person's punishment is not commensurate with the crime, it's perfectly possible they may not learn their lesson and commit that crime again. Also, if a person commits a dishonest act, whether they get caught or not, unless the circumstances surrounding the dishonest act are changed, the dishonesty may continue. Here's a very hypothetical situation: Let's say this person is an employee of the U.S. Mint and earns $6.00 per hour. The location where this person works has no cameras and this person has unrestricted and unsupervised contact with millions of dollars daily. Forgive me but sometimes, not often, but sometimes I get these bursts of logic where I can't help but question things, which I consider incredibly stupid and one of those incredibly stupid things I've noticed is the practice that the U.S. Mint has of actually shredding old money. I assume that given the amount of money they produce, several millions of dollars can be eliminated at any one time. I may be alone here but isn't old money just as valuable as new money? I understand that if the bills are mutilated and unusable, they should be destroyed. I also understand about the increased

4

difficulty in counterfeiting but couldn't that be fixed by more diligent counterfeit screening procedures - and not to go off on a tangent here but what about the homeless situation? To alleviate the problem of them panhandling and annoying the fuck out of everybody, what's so entirely wrong with giving them a few thousand here and there, while teaching them about investing and monitoring their spending habits? If you really sit down and think about it, the majority of homeless are displaced because of bad budgeting. I know there are the obvious exceptions such as fire, natural disasters, unmotivated drug addicts and just plain lazy people but if everyone who had any type of income were taught how to save ten or twenty percent each time they received income, homelessness would be nowhere near the problem it is now. Anyway this person who makes this very unlivable wage and sees all of this money going to waste also sees the opportunity to supplement his income. He takes a couple of hundred dollar bills from each batch of money to be destroyed and nobody is the wiser. Time passes and nothing is said about the missing money. My question is other than this man's conscience, what is actually there to make him return the stolen money or to prevent him from stealing again? If on the other hand, a person commits an act of dishonesty and gets caught, whether by authorities or by his conscience and is traumatized to the point of lifelong memory or regret, chances of the act recurring will significantly decrease. Now continuing with the hypothetical, let's say someone purchases a new Rolls Royce, 2010 edition and two days after its purchase, it is stolen and totaled. The authorities eventually catch the perpetrator, charge him with petit larceny and sentence him to one weekend in jail. Chances are when this person is released; he will more than likely commit the same crime again and again and again. If however, the perpetrator was to be charged with a slightly more severe penalty such as death or a minimum mandatory sentence of thirty years without the possibility of parole, I'm pretty sure that soon, car theft would be a thing of the past. In regards to the once a cheat, always a cheat thing, if someone cheats on another and their partner chooses to stay with them, to alleviate the possibility of them doing it again, one should let the punishment not only fit but exceed the parameters of the crime. Many people will agree that revenge is the best remedy in most situations but sometimes revenge can cause more damage than the original transgression. The thing with revenge is that is it often the first thought of action when infidelity is committed. It is rarely the best option however because revenge can start a cycle which will most likely never end or if it does end, will end with somebody dying or catching a sexually transmitted disease. If the consequences of repeating an action are so severe that a person would not want to risk them, the likelihood of them repeating that action will be significantly diminished, if not eradicated. There are some people who feel that if they were to catch their mate cheating, a suitable punishment would be to end the relationship. There are some people who feel that if they were to catch their significant others with a member of the opposite sex, a just punishment would be bodily harm, as in cutting off a piece of that person's anatomy. There are even some others who feel that if the fidelity band is broken, the only thing that will satisfy is capital punishment. Ending a relationship because of infidelity is one of the most favorite things of many people. When a person cheats and gets caught, the other can say 'phew, I've got my walking papers, now I can fool around with whoever I want without feeling guilty' or they can say 'I was smothered or unhappy in the relationship and needed a way out.' That way out will be the partner's infidelity. Everything in life comes with some sort of an out clause or some kind of forgiving – something to basically say 'it's okay, it happens to everybody' or 'I can cover my actions by using this defense.' Religious people have what's called backsliding. Backsliding is what happens when somebody who has given their life to their chosen higher power falls back into the type of life they lived before they made the decision to give their life to their chosen higher power. Backsliding has been used and accepted as a viable excuse due to the fact that people are human and people make mistakes. Married people have divorce. Divorce is what happens when there is no more making up. Divorce is making corrections to a bad choice. Divorce is what comes into play after the annulment grace period passes. Politicians plead the Fifth Amendment. This basically means 'I'm not going to explain myself and I don't have to because of the possibility of self incrimination. These are put in place basically because again everybody in this world is human, which means everybody is capable of failure. Most normal relationships, meaning between two people, were meant to be exclusive, however lives were not. Though a person may devote his or her life to one person, that does not mean everyone else in the world should be excluded nor does that mean a person in a relationship will equally reciprocate the other's feelings. Ever hear of 'mama's baby, papa's maybe?' well in relationships it's often 'mama's devoted, papa's corroded.' This is why I believe people in relationships should never lose touch or try never to lose touch with certain contacts from their past. Friendships made before relationships should not be made to end because of those relationships. Past friendships should also <u>NEVER</u> be hidden from present relationships. Annulments fall under the same theory. It allows one to get a feel for the person they are involved with but allows them a way out if they are not completely satisfied after a certain amount of time. In most committed relationships, excluding marriage or should I say a real marriage, people will often keep at least one other on the side, in the pocket or in close proximity just in case the relationship doesn't exactly work out.

Continuing with the above example – there are some people who will change the circumstances surrounding their lives to accommodate them. Let's say a person who is raised in the catholic faith gets married at say twenty years old and he or she stays married for all of seven months. If ten years later, after that person matures and learns to base relationships on things other than sexual attraction, they find someone who they are interested in, they will not be able to marry due to the restrictions set forth by their religion. Problem? For some maybe but not these people. What these people do in their never ending quest for self gratification and happiness is forsake their own religion, a few even going so far as to imitate the idea behind some internet chat rooms, where if you cannot find one you are completely comfortable with or one which is to your liking, you can create your own. Many relationships that go through infidelity can be saved but BOTH partners must be willing to work at saving it. If one partner is unhappy and just drifting along, going through the motions, then the first transgression will more than likely be the last. Going back to the example about anatomical separation, it sounds like fun but that will more than likely invite legal involvement. Nobody wants that. Capital punishment in regards to payback for someone breaking your heart is something I think almost everyone who has been on the receiving end of an affair has thought of at least once – but again possible or should I say definite legal action. A lesson is something people learn, most times willingly. Killing because of infidelity, as fun and as justifiable as it may sound will not teach anything to the person who committed the indiscretion. Why? They're dead. I've heard more times than I can remember, Too err is human – To forgive, divine. I don't know about any of you but I haven't met any people who would fall into the category of divine. If there is such a category, however I strongly believe its presence would be severely overshadowed by the human factor. Personally, I do not advocate letting anybody off the hook if they've hurt you, especially if they've hurt your heart but when it comes to vengeance, do something, which will make them remember – not something, which will land you in jail. Do something that whenever they even THINK about hurting another human being, will send your face screaming into their memory. In conclusion, as with everything in life, there needs to be some sort of balance. Too soft and people may never stop their transgressions, hence giving credibility to the once a cheat, always a cheat thing. Too severe and people may completely scare away the ones they are trying teach the lesson to.

Chapter Ten
Target Markets

People use what's called targeting or target markets to find certain types of people to cheat with. As in business, certain companies will advertise to target areas to attract a certain customer base. For instance, certain retailers in some neighborhoods will only carry a certain type of beverage or even a certain type of ice cream. Other retailers in other neighborhoods will not. For example: in all my years and in all of my travels, I have yet to see malt liquor (which is sold very frequently in minority neighborhoods) being sold in or at the same rates as in more affluent (non minority) neighborhoods. I will not focus on why I think this is so as much as the fact that it just is. I have found out that the same thing is true for certain foods. Retailers will not sell what's commonly known or accepted as food for a certain race in neighborhoods not of that race. Example – certain types of soul food cannot be found in certain suburban markets. I remember spending one summer away from the inner city, still in New York, yet an area, which would be classified by most as suburbia. One day, a few friends and I decided to make a big dinner for the ladies of the house – you know the ole southern, Sunday, after church, family type of meals. When we went to the mall, I only wish I had a camera to record the expressions on the faces of the supermarket employees as they tried to figure out what chitterlings actually were. Now even though soul food has been historically linked to minorities, more specifically, African Americans and even though this particular suburb had its fair share of people of color, not much soul food could be found. I won't mention where this place is actually located because I don't want to bring any negative attention to it nor do I want people to know where I occasionally hang out but it had shown me that everybody cannot find everything, everywhere. It had also taken me quite a few years to realize that crème brulee was a type of ice cream, which not only tasted good but was readily available, in large quantities, just a few miles outside of my neighborhood. An inquisitive person such as me always wondered why that was. Even books, which cater to a predominantly white audience, are almost never sold in predominantly black book stores or in locations, which cater primarily to black people. If the target or intended market is white, the belief is that sales will not do as well in non white areas. (kinda the reasoning behind why I put white folks on the cover of my first book.) For some reason or other, the mass misconception is that if a person puts out a book with a white person or with white people on the cover, the book is intended for all. If on the other hand, a person puts out a book where a person of color who has not or is not currently maintaining celebrity status, then the book is only intended for people of color. Isn't that strange? (That's right; the Caucasian people were strictly a marketing strategy.) Now continuing along those lines, I find that many people in this world have their own target markets when it comes to whom they date as well as whom they choose when planning an affair. In my first publication, I tried to explain that the process of cheating was not a simple one. I'm finding now that more and more people are taking that philosophy to heart. Some people will study the demographics, finances and education of a person or persons, and then use the results to determine if they are compatible mates for an affair. Some of these people will focus on how well these individuals can maintain a particular secret before jumping into bed with them. Poor people have target markets as well as not so poor people. Poor people or should I say less affluent individuals often share in what's called the 'crack head mentality' meaning they will do 'not anything but a lot of things' for money. I have nothing personal against people who abuse drugs because most of them are just so much fun to hang out with and they, just like everybody else in this world have vices. Theirs just happen to be drugs. Some people in this world just have a knack for spotting these crack head mentality having individuals and use money to lure them into a sexual relationship as a drug dealer would use drugs or the promise of to lure a drug addict. Sometimes it's more than a 'knack' to identify certain types of people. Sometimes it's an actual psychology to be able to decipher which people have real problems, which people have a couple of issues and which people are just in need of a hug. Relationships are often comprised of three parts; one part conversation, one part stimulation and one part manipulation. This is the thinking behind how many pimps attract and manipulate their employees. They just seem to be able to target women who are in dire need of care and direction. The poor or less affluent people will be the target market of some sexual sickos with money. The ones with money know the ones without most likely share the crack head mentality and will do what has to be done to get that money. It must be stated that many of these less affluent people are not by definition prostitutes; they are just people who involve themselves in relationships where their finances take a higher priority than their feelings. In other words, they target the rich or more affluent people the same way the more affluent people do them. Target markets extend way beyond the amount of money a person does or does not have. They can include certain races as well as certain ages. Races are targeted due to beliefs, fallacies or even experiences people may have had in the past. For instance, if a person of African American descent had provided you with the most orgasmic experience of recent memory, chances are you may be more inclined to believe that other African Americans possess the same type of skill at that particular endeavor. This is the belief but not always the case. Unlike as with food, people of the same race and their abilities will vary greatly. Ages are targeted because the big belief is that specific ages can enhance the sexual experience. Many women in their mid to late thirties have reputations for being more sexually active than at most other times in their lives. Many young men have a reputation for being the same way during their late teens. Beliefs such as these lead to May – December relationships as well as relationships, which focus on little other than money and sex.

The idea of target markets basically stems from the belief that everybody has a preference. If this were not so, every man would or could comfortably sleep with any and every woman and every woman could do the same. People who are viewed as repulsively obese would be just as desirable as those seen as supermodels. But this isn't so. When relating to infidelity, people who have been cheated on often feel that a man will sleep with anybody who allows him to and to an extent this is true but for the most part there are certain people that attract another and these are the types of individuals that couples should steer clear from. This does not mean to say that if a man has a fancy for white girls 5'8 150lbs with a tan, that he will never be interested in somebody of a different race. It means that more attention should be paid when this type of individual is around. When a man for instance is caught in the act of infidelity, it is often extremely difficult for forgiveness to enter the equation because the woman who was cheated on will most often have doubts about his future fidelity and fears about the opposite sex in general. But people need to know what others have an attraction to or desire for to begin with. As stated before this does not mean to say that if a man were to cheat with a slim woman one time, the next time he would not cheat with someone heavy. Physical appearance is only one of the many factors which perpetuate an affair. A skinny person could create the same kind of emotional connection that is had between the significant other and the spouse just as someone on the opposite end of the scale could. A person can sometimes look at oneself to get an idea of what the significant others target market may be and they can do this easily because many times what a person finds attractive or appealing in the one they deal with, they may also find the same thing appealing in someone else even if only for a short period of time.

Chapter Eleven
Options, Perceptions and Misconceptions

There are three things, which have heavily contributed to the scourge of infidelity since its onset. They are options, perceptions and misconceptions. Options contribute to infidelity in two ways – too many of them and too few. When a person is young, undisciplined and carefree, they have many choices, especially in relationships. They have the choice to be in one or not, to be faithful while in one or to be the biggest philanderer ever created. When a young person has too many options, they cheat basically to expel their excess energy. In short, the idea of infidelity is pretty much equivalent to a person's level of morals. When a person gets older however, as with most things in life, their options become somewhat limited. They have to then work within their means. Most people in this world become smarter as they age and realize that they are unable to do the things they did when they were young or if they are still able, they are not able to do them as well. These people, when older, also realize that promiscuity has its consequences. The older a person gets, the more he or she may realize that terminal sexual diseases are a very real occurrence and that many commitments are only as good as the fidelity two people share. When people mature, their physical features are not as attractive or as firm and are not as magnetic to the opposite sex as when they were young. A person's options as far as the opposite sex will decrease with age mainly because we live in what's called an appearance based society. If one is in a relationship and the relationship is not going well, that person of a certain moral fortitude will more than likely cheat but will have a harder time because they will not have such a broad spectrum of choices as say during teenage years.

A young child, who has a multitude of toys, may one day and for no reason at all, destroy many of them with the attitude of 'its okay, I've got more.' If not corrected this attitude can grow into adulthood, as well as into relationships. There are a lot of people in relationships who share this attitude because they think that since there are so many others who find them attractive, they can treat people however they want and for as long as they want. These people don't yet realize that with increased age come decreased opportunities and/or options. Opportunities for additional partners in relationships will always present themselves however the caliber of those opportunities or the reasons why they want you may not be what you expect. With infidelity, on the side of the philanderer, a person has but two simple options, whether to commit the transgressions or not. On the side of the innocent party, a person basically has but two simple options also, whether to accept them or not. Also on the side of the innocent party are a couple of other options relating to what a person can do in the face of infidelity and those are to let it affect that person or not. Infidelity and its effects can wear on a person for a long time. The choice to move on after an affair is not an easy one but a necessary one. A grudge, brought on by infidelity can last the entire length of a relationship or the length of a life. The memory of an affair has the wondrous and almost miraculous capability to transcend and outlast almost any other type of memory. A person can steal your paycheck as well as steal your car. The victims of these crimes may dwell on them for years but what will happen more than likely is the incidents will eventually be forgotten or if not forgotten, then remembered with less animosity than when first perpetrated. Depending upon the individual, the events may even be quickly forgiven but infidelity is much different. Infidelity deals with the heart. Crimes of the heart hold a much greater penalty than those of other types. People will try their best to have prosecuted the ones who steal their paychecks and/or cars but rarely will they resort to capital punishment. Someone breaks a heart, especially because of infidelity and people have little trouble throwing aside common sense, logic and reasoning to grab a pistol and attempt to blow the perpetrating parties ass off the face of the earth. People can better deal with someone breaking their heart by saying 'I don't love you anymore' as opposed to an outright affair. Whenever infidelity occurs, it is viewed as a direct attack on the other person in the relationship. It's always 'you cheated on me!' or 'you hurt me!' Infidelity is never thought of as one person falls out of love, then falls in love with someone else before breaking up – even if that is the actual case. People don't forget cheating, they either accept it and deal with it or they don't. If a person finds himself or herself involved in a committed relationship, which they are not completely ready for they may feel trapped. This feeling too may limit the number of options that particular person may have. That person may cheat as a way of experiencing freedom or as a means of escape.

Perception – the process of using the senses to acquire information about the surrounding environment or situation. Perception contributes to infidelity not always by truth but many times by what people believe to be true. If one person believes infidelity to be prevalent in his relationship, that belief, if unchallenged, will destroy the relationship. For instance, if a man feels his wife, whom he loves is cheating on him, he may in an attempt to heal his hurt, cheat on her as well as cheat with as many women as he can find. The cause of this could be nothing more than one of those situations, which resemble infidelity, like her being overly tired or just not in the mood or being overly friendly with the opposite sex. If one partner in a relationship perceives the other as being satisfied, he or she will continue to act as if that partner is indeed satisfied in the relationship. The other partner may in fact be satisfied or may just be acting on the other's perceptions to lull their partner into a sense of false security, so that they will have room to cheat. The wonderful and at the same time disheartening thing about perception is that everybody's is different. While one person can perceive a situation as dangerous, another can perceive the exact same situation as reason for concern and still another may be able to perceive that situation as non threatening. Going back to the example about satisfaction, a great deal of people believe that when it comes to sex, no matter how it's done, as long as its done, both parties enjoy it. This is <u>Mistaken Perception #1.</u> Many people will risk as well as put aside their potential happiness and satisfaction all to save the feelings of their partner. They will do this because they do not wish to upset the illusion of happiness, which has been created by their silence. If some of these people were to actually voice their dissatisfaction, their partners, instead of trying to understand, would more than likely take it as a personal attack and respond negatively. The biggest 'for instance' I can give is the sexual performance thing. Men, for the most part, think that whenever a woman says 'ow, you hurt me!' that means the man did a good job. When the few women who would actually complain, do and say 'you're doing it wrong,' or 'I'm supposed to enjoy sex too' instead of using that criticism as a reference point to improve their performance, the men often get upset. This applies to both sexes because often there is what's called sexual incompatibility. This is where a man's plumbing is not always sufficient for the home it will be fitted into. Women love to talk about this especially when they break up from this type of union but it must be stated that every size is not meant for every occasion. In sexual incompatibility cases people stay together because they fear the truth. The men fear being labeled too small and the women fear being labeled too big and this is because men will be thought of as inadequate and women will be thought of as whores. They too often use the line 'I love the person, so we'll make the sex work. That is a very noble thought and gesture but when these women break up and start male bashing, especially about the size matters thing, who was really wrong for staying involved, them or the men? 'Too many people in this world have what's called a 'if it ain't broke, don't fix it mentality.' This way of thinking is good for certain things but what folks in a relationship need to understand is that something is always broke. There is no perfect relationship. A lot of people will wait until something happens, which causes an undue amount of drama, then attempt to work it out. This is what's called having a reactive approach to problems. There is such a thing as having a proactive approach to problems or doing what's known as preventative maintenance. This is where every so often; you work on small, seemingly non existent problems so that they don't become big, overwhelming problems. When I say something is 'always broke' in a relationship, I do not mean that your relationship is not working, I mean that there is something, which can always be worked on or improved. The interpretation of one's perceptions can and always will mess up a relationship. This is because the thought process of some people in relationships resembles not 'I know what you think' but more 'I think I know what you think.' This is basically the same as dealing with someone based on an assumption. This is also where on going and open communication in relationships helps immensely. What people need to do, instead of thinking they know what their partners think, is ask them – and not ask them with a 'I wanna hear any and everything you have to say to me, just as long as it doesn't upset me' type of mindset but with an open mind, one that is willing to work at changing any deficiency, which may be found. Here's a question to ponder, do you ever notice how some people view younger folks having fun? When I say fun, I mean the way young people, especially teenagers act with their undisciplined, total disregard for manners and authority? I have seen people refer to them as the worst of creation, yet many of these people forget that they themselves were at one time young. I find that many of these undisciplined, worst of creation teens are going through a phase, which many of us adults have traveled through at one time or another during our lives. And many adults will now argue that those years, while maybe not the best, were among some of the most fun times in their lives or at least in recent memory. What happens after that phase is these kids grow up, get jobs, learn what is expected of them from society at large and are then conditioned into becoming the boring and lifeless, walking ruts known today as most adults. Now to look at this from a relationship standpoint; many relationships start out young, exciting, a little reckless and somewhat annoying to older people and those not in relationships. After a few years, once the new relationship euphoria wears down and people become more mature and start to really plan for their future, many younger relationships seem annoying or not completely understood to them. I've noticed that once people change their way of thinking, they change how they view relationships. Something a person does at sixteen, which is fun can at forty be looked upon as dangerous. For instance, growing up I can remember my friends and I throwing bottles at one another. As long as no one got hurt, it was considered fun. However, now that I'm all grown up I realize that to every action there is a consequence and consequences are not always positive. I realize now that throwing those bottles back then could have resulted in someone losing an eye or someone bleeding to death from a glass shard. That's the one problem with wisdom, sometimes it takes too damn long to arrive.

Continuing with perception and at the risk of sounding like a total perv, there are many people who perceive or interpret the art of masturbation as less socially acceptable than the art of cheating - the lesser of two evils, if you will. These people believe that fornication and infidelity are two separate violations when it comes to betrayal in a relationship. Now while both of these things are morally wrong, religiously wrong and pretty much socially inadequate, many in relationships find ways in which to navigate their presence. What's funny about this is that most women will consider masturbation by a man they're involved with a form of infidelity, which in their mind is equal to sleeping with someone of the opposite sex. And they may believe it's due to men not wanting to have sex with them instead of believing that the men actually having a 'problem' themselves. Most men on the other hand will justify the act of self gratification by saying it's better than actually going out and having a physical affair with someone outside of the relationship and they may justify the reason for it as anything from not a high enough level of intimacy in the relationship to addiction. Levels of intimacy and addiction have always been reason for an affair, whether too high a stratum – as with a young man who has superhuman levels of testosterone or too low a level of intimacy – as with the part of the unfulfilled spouse. Addiction to masturbation can come about just like any other kind of addiction. People are prone to being attracted to certain things. Cocaine can become addictive to one person after only one try. The next person can do it one hundred times, then give it up cold turkey. Masturbation can be just as addicting or just as easy to give up. The reason a lot of men seem to indulge in this practice as much as they do is because they want the sensation of anytime intimacy without the repercussions of constantly sleeping around with different women. The men will also reason that there is no chance for sexually transmitted diseases or no chance for negative interaction from the third party in an affair, if there ever was one. Masturbation has benefits for both sexes. It often benefits a woman the way a prostitute would benefit a man – the bottom line for both being satisfaction and fantasy. Women often resort to masturbation, not because they are sex crazed nymphomaniacs, as many men would like to believe but often because they are not satisfied with the initial act of sex – so instead of pulling out an oversized penis shaped piece of polyurethane, possibly and potentially crushing the man's ego, the woman will most often pretend that her solo sex act is being used to further enhance the sex act between the two. The perception from people outside of the relationship would most likely be that since one or both of the parties have to resort to singular or separate stimulation, there is something wrong with the level of intimacy within the relationship. Now even though self stimulation does have a negative connotation as well as negative history associated with its practice, it has also been known to enhance the sexual experience. But as stated before a person's perceptions will always make or break the legitimacy surrounding another's actions.

When it comes to the way some men try and attract the attention of a woman with whom they find interest, many people are often perturbed, especially that particular woman. There is a 'practice' if you will, which entails many men using a cat call or more specifically, the psst (punctured tired sound). The general consensus or perception is that men who use that tactic are dogs and have no redeeming qualities with which the woman may ever find interest. It's not thought of that maybe the particular man didn't notice the woman until she was too far away too get her attention by waving and he doesn't want to draw more attention to her than what's necessary. It's not even thought of that that particular man may be everything the woman is looking for, just a bad conversation initiator. The general perception quite often includes 'if a person is not everything I want from the beginning of the relationship, they never will be.' This is one of the problems with perception – it is quite often like first impression, which is many times wrong or if not wrong, then not as complete as second or third impressions.

Another good example about perceptions would have to be the way people equate an individual's line of work with their actual personality or disposition. I've seen it happen all too often where a police officer is automatically judged as bad just because he's a cop or he's an aggressive, mean cop because he's big in stature. There are gentle giants who are large in stature that wouldn't hurt a fly just as there are those with the so called napoleon inferiority complex who feel that because they are smaller than most they have to be meaner than most. And still another example is the security officer who is automatically judged as stupid or not as intelligent as other employees just because of his position. Countless people will walk into an establishment looking for assistance and bypass the lowly security officer (whose job by the way, is to provide information & assistance). They will then say 'oh, he's just security – he doesn't know anything.' Granted, many times security personnel are hired for one specific purpose and that purpose usually is to prevent theft as well as to prevent loss of life and property. Sometimes they are not told about the day to day operations of certain establishments in which they work. Sometimes these security personnel work for a contract organization, which has hundreds of different sites and they often bump security personnel to different sites every day, so it is possible for a new officer to have just arrived five minutes before someone with an attitude asks an otherwise relatively simple question like 'where's the bathroom' and the security officer not to know. Unfortunately, many times security personnel know much more than the attitude having people think as well as more than they know themselves but these ignorant people let their perceptions guide their beliefs. These types of perceptions are based on many things such as education, parental influence and even prior dealings with certain types of individuals. If a man for instance was taught by his father that a woman should always be ready to have sex, with the obvious monthly exception and of course when she is mad – chances are if there was ever a time other than the two exceptions stated above where the woman was not willing to have sex, he would more than likely reason she is being unfaithful. If by prior experience that man has been led to believe women who dress provocatively are more sexually experimental or are more likely to cheat, that belief would carry on into subsequent relationships.

Continuing with the abundance of incorrect perceptions, I find that many people in this world mistakenly associate a person's abilities with their appearance. They believe that if a person looks innocent, they are. They believe that if a person looks dumb, same thing applies. The problem with some people is that when they are young and their bodies are tight and juicy and delectable and whatever else, many times, those minds are still developing. With a lot of people, when their minds are at the optimum level for understanding life and relationships and what they both entail, the bodies of these enlightened folk are often overweight, outta shape and generally not that great. What's true and sad at the same time is that few people in this world actually want to be involved with the heavyset, ugly, smart person. Just like with an employment situation, if a person graduated from an Ivy league institution, in the top percentile of his or her class but was fat and refused to wear business attire or keep a decent, regular hairstyle, they would be offered many positions but few where their potential co-workers have to fit into the above realm of business world normalcy. It doesn't matter what you know or what you can or have accomplished as much as what you look like. I guess this is just one more of the disadvantages of living in an appearance based society. These people don't believe or refuse to accept the fact that as I said in the first chapter of this book, 'Deception is arguably one of man's greatest weapons.' When a person is in a relationship, they are basically at the mercy of their partner. A person can have nothing but honest, good and true intentions toward their partner but they are putting themselves 'out there' so to speak, when they expect to get those things back. People need to know and realize that there are some people in this world who are just out here to hurt others, no matter how good and true their partners are to them. (This is the cloud of complacency many people refuse to believe exists) There are a variety of reasons why as well as a variety of methods but the point I am basically trying to make is everybody is not who they portray themselves to be. Too many people in this world take what I'm trying to say out of context. I do not mean for anybody out here to stop trusting their mates, I just want people to learn to keep their eyes open. There is so much deception in this world; it can most accurately be compared with air. They are both everywhere you go. The bad part about this is that in a relationship, it's rare to be able to put all of your trust in your partner. So much of the truth sounds like lies nowadays a person has to lower their defenses and basically become overwhelmingly vulnerable if they are willing to risk a relationship. If you don't already know, let me be the first one to tell you, it's not easy, especially when people have been deceived by almost every faction of society. Policemen, firemen, priests, parents and family members, it leaves a person wondering whom can they really trust? With the constant media bombardment of negativity toward these groups and more, it's only natural that a person would be apprehensive when weighing the options of a relationship. Here's a question many people (especially women) have a interesting time answering; Why would a man feel the need to cheat on a woman who everybody outside of their relationship thinks is the best thing God has ever created? The first thing I've noticed woman saying in response to this question is 'he's a dog!' or 'he ain't shit!' as well as an entire truckload full of male badgering excuses catered to making the woman appear as if she's the completely innocent victim. Two popular reasons many people seem to overlook are one, because she's a witch (yes I substituted the b for a w) and two, quite possibly because of perceptions. Perceptions will cause people to look at and judge only the side, which is shown, instead of what could be considered the big picture. While the circle of influence at a person's job can be convinced beyond a shadow of a doubt that that person is only capable of doing good and wonderful things, they might not be able to envision the home side, where that person nags consistently or doesn't talk to their significant other or doesn't allow their significant other to have sex with them or a whole list of things the office does not see. Perceptions are never a reliable screening method because again, they are the same as first impressions, which are far too often misleading.

When it comes to some relationships, members of the opposite sex become taboo to people in that relationship. The general perception is if a woman is married, she is not able or no longer able to associate freely with members of the opposite sex unless her husband is present. The same holds true for a married man. These people can no longer have friends unless they are friends of both parties, the husband and the wife and of the same individual sex as that of either the husband or wife. This is a great rule of thumb because on the one hand it cuts down on potential intimacies between a significant other and a stranger. It can be a potentially bad thing on the other hand because it may increase the possibility of more 'personalized affection' between one of those friends

– thereby causing the inevitable breakup, which will more than likely cause the dissolution of the friendship. The big perception is 'men and women can't be friends.' That perception continues to grow into 'if they are friends, they must at one time or another have had a sexual relationship, they are presently having a sexual relationship or one of them wants to pursue a sexual relationship in the near future.' This perception stems from infidelity's history of destroying friendships. When people are young as boys and girls, they become friends. They grow older, then friends become boyfriend and girlfriend. Time progresses and boyfriend and girlfriend eventually become husband and wife. If there's an affair, which destroys the relationship between husband & wife, nine times out of ten, it will also destroy the friendship. There are some exceptions where people can remain friends after being in a relationship but the transferring of feelings, which are shared between lovers to the feelings, which are shared between friends will make that journey exceptionally difficult.

Misconceptions – this is the alter ego of the above paragraph about perceptions. Misconceptions are the things, which cause people to get into fake relationships. They cause people to make judgments on beliefs, which are not completely accurate or understood. Many people in this world are for lack of a better phrase, full of something. They <u>know</u> full well what they look like to themselves. However, they only <u>think</u> they know how they appear to others. Unattractive people know whether or not they fit into society's accepted criteria regarding what is 'pretty or handsome' even though many of them will most often classify themselves as 'average.' Attractive people are pretty much the same. When asked about their appearance, unless an attractive person is humble, they will more likely say they are attractive. If they are humble, they are likely to downplay their looks. People who are 'average looking' can go either way, depending on their perceptions or self esteem. The misconceptions start when a person shows interest in someone one second longer than what that person is used to. For instance, let's say a person who is classified by much of society as unattractive, only has relationships for short periods of time and often starts those relationships the same day he or she meets someone. If they were to meet someone who only wanted to indulge in a physical relationship with them but who took the time to meet them, get to know about their likes and dislikes and made daily contact, whether by phone, email or actual physical interaction, they would more than likely be under the misconception that that person actually liked them more than that person actually does. These misconceptions cause people to 'act' a way they think they are supposed to instead of acting how they normally would.

Misconceptions contribute to cheating in other ways too. For instance, people can see a couple having a loud disagreement and think that that couple is unhappy. People will get this wrong idea because they do not realize that not everybody has the same criteria regarding what constitutes a happy relationship as they themselves do. Some people like to argue and yell and just be socially inept – and not only that, these people are many times just as happy as the people who look at them and think that they are not. Misconceptions also contribute to infidelity because some people mistakenly think that the only thing necessary to rectify the problems an unhappy union is or might be experiencing is a healthy dose of sex. Not always. Some couples need therapy, some couples need space and true, in some rare instances, problems can be rectified with greater or more frequent intimate sessions – but not always with somebody new. This type of misconception is basically the mistaken perception of the people outside of the relationship. It can be viewed as a matter of perspective, the same way there are two different views with people inside a forest looking out and people outside a forest looking in. They can both say they see trees and they can even say they see some of the same trees but they will not see all of the trees the same. If there is no sex being had in the relationship for whatever reason and every other aspect of the relationship is going well and one party in the relationship desires sex, it may, in some rare instances, actually help the relationship to stay together. I'm not saying if your partner doesn't give you any, it's okay to go out and cheat. I'm saying that it may be possible for one indiscretion to not totally cause the breakdown of everything you and your significant other have worked for. Satisfying a sexual urge can sometimes provide

18

the temporary and necessary release, which would otherwise cause arguments and unhappy feelings. There is always a potential disadvantage in this situation because a person may enjoy the outside sex a little too much and desire its continuation.

People love to talk about their relationships, sometimes more than what's advisable. If people who are on the receiving end of these conversations believe a relationship is in jeopardy, they may interpret the conversation as an invitation to a relationship. Let's say Kim & Ryan are married. They both have a mutual friend named Tasha. One day or maybe on several days Kim tells Tasha how many arguments she & Ryan are having. Tasha may take it upon herself to play sex psychologist and try to help the relationship by sleeping with Ryan. Ryan may be a faithful husband and initially may reject the advances of Tasha but Tasha may use whatever information she has received from Kim to help her cause. For example, Kim can confide in Tasha that Ryan doesn't have sex as much as she would like or that the bills are never paid on time. Tasha can switch up that conversation so that it sounds as if Kim has said Ryan has a little dick or that he is not satisfying her. She could also say that Ryan does not have the type of money needed to sufficiently sustain her lifestyle. If Ryan finds out that Kim has told Tasha certain private things about their relationship, he may feel betrayed and sleep with Tasha or someone else as payback. Let's switch up the scenario a little bit. Let's say

Ryan was the one who confided in Tasha about his problems with Kim. Since men have a history for initiating infidelity, Tasha may think that since Ryan is unhappy, he is either planning to leave Kim or attempting to initiate an affair.

Continuing with misconceptions, a person can be nice to another because niceness is in their nature meaning that is how he or she was raised. The bad part about that is that another person can read more into something than what actually exists. One person being nice can be misconstrued by another into 'she likes me' or 'she wants to give me some booty.' This is sometimes but not always the case. Sometimes people need harsh truth. Sometimes people need explicitness. Sometimes they need to hear 'no motherfucker, I do not like you. My husband and I are just having a few problems, which we'll get over without you and your dick, thank you very much.' One of the problems, which help misconceptions continue to grow and destroy relationships is that people have become too sensitive. They don't want to hurt the feelings of other people so they often downplay their own emotions. In relationships, sensitivity is rarely good in places other than the bedroom. People in relationships sometimes need to be brutally honest, especially when it comes to misconceptions. They need to be tactful but they need to be brutal at the same time. If a person is not pleasing another in the bedroom and they are too sensitive or too fearful to hurt that person's feelings with the truth, they will more than likely continue to sacrifice their pleasure, possibly leading them to eventually seek pleasure elsewhere.

Misconceptions also cause or contribute to cheating with the help of those situations, which resemble infidelity. Those situations are plentiful, stretching from overhearing incriminating phone calls, to unexplained absences to observing one's significant other with members of the opposite sex, whom they do not know. Another one of the things, which fuel misconceptions, is the fact that many times they go unchallenged. Misconceptions are just like unproven statements or lies. An unproven statement is nothing more than someone mentioning a fact such as it's raining without someone else looking outside to verify that fact. The misconception comes in when someone does look outside and notices it's not raining – to which the first person may respond 'I said it was raining, I didn't say where.' This could be considered trickery on the side of one but it is still a misconception on the side of the other. A lie as we all know usually comes about for two main reasons. Those reasons are to protect feelings and to escape consequences. There are plenty of reasons why people lie but I'd like to focus on these two. A helpful lie, one, which protects feelings, can go unchallenged and cause little or no detriment to a relationship. This type of lie can be anything from a spouse receiving positive feedback regarding an art class project to that same spouse desiring affirmation on his or her own intelligence. Lying about an art class project can have positive results because even if you know in your heart that something your spouse has created is butt ugly, you can give them positive reinforcement, leading them to continue and ultimately improve. Positive reinforcement is often a pretty way of saying lie. If that spouse were to tell the truth and say honey, I think your art project is butt ugly, the spouse on the receiving end may give up his or her dream of being the next Picasso. A person can be extremely tactful and tasteful in why the art project is not to their liking but the end result is all that really matters.

Some people do not finish high school and many times these people get involved with others who have. Knowing that many opportunities will be limited for the non grads, they may often feel that they are not as intelligent as their peers with diplomas or GED's. The spouse without a high school education may ask for reassurance from his significant other that although he dropped out, he is still smart enough to compete with those who didn't. Again, like the above situation, it can be handled two ways; truthful or helpful. If the situation is handled truthfully, to wit: 'no honey, you are not as smart as you think you are. You need to go back to school, otherwise you won't amount to anything' feelings will definitely be perturbed. If however, the situation was handled with positive reinforcement, to wit: 'yes honey, you are as smart as your high school diploma having peers, you've just been educated differently.' You can then throw in the old 'they're book smart but you're street smart' thing. Plus for a finishing touch, you can always add 'if you go back to school and you don't need to but if you do, you will be twice as smart as they think they are.' This situation will become helpful, possibly causing the dropout to re attend school and possibly garnering the knowledge they would have gained, had they stayed in school in the first place. The other type of lie, the one, which allows a person to escape consequences, is just the opposite. This type of lie can cause great damage and hardship to a relationship. Examples of these types of lies are traffic stop fabrications, 'I was late because' and the ever popular 'he or she was my cousin.' These lies, with the exception of the traffic stop can go unchallenged but they can and often will eventually cause some sort of detriment to a relationship. Lying to a traffic cop for instance, is almost instinctive when some people get pulled over. Now a well fabricated story can help certain people out of that situation but what if the reason given for the excessive speed was because the driver was on the way to the hospital to see an injured or sick family member. And what if the officer was in the mood and position to play Good Samaritan, meaning he was nice enough to escort the driver to the hospital. Whatever lie the driver told and whatever leeway the driver received would be null and void once they reached the hospital or once the driver decided to fess up. Things like this sometimes happen due to fate or due to John Q Murphy and his law. The other two examples 'I was late because' and 'he or she was my cousin' can directly affect a relationship because they are harder to prove and most times include contact with another person. The 'I was late because' excuse usually encompasses traffic, work and/or another person. The cousin excuse is due to an actual relative or due to someone the significant other is probably sleeping around with. The difference between the types of lies is that the first couple, the art project and education are basically opinions and opinions are never wrong. Everybody sees something different, as with the art project and everybody in this world learns differently even though their methods of education and training may have been similar. The second examples, the 'I was late because' and 'she was my cousin' are facts. Facts, even though extensive digging may be necessary, are able to be proven or disputed. People bank on other people's acceptance of any run of the mill excuse or they bank on people's reluctance to do any fact checking. This is how misconceptions can help and hurt relationships.

In conclusion, it must be stated that cheating is not normal behavior. It is not 'natural' nor is it something 'everybody does.' Cheating is what some misguided individuals deem necessary retribution or what some issue having individuals consider fun. In a relationship, there are many unwritten laws. Forgiveness is one of those laws, which is an absolute necessity for longevity in the union. If a person in a relationship cannot forgive the other's indiscretions, the relationship is doomed from day one. Let's look at the bullying example. If a person was beat on, harassed or excessively ridiculed during school years and that person never properly dealt with the bully or dealt with the problems, which the bullying may have caused, that person may have hatred towards the bully or fears toward others, for life. In a relationship, if a person doesn't deal with infidelity, whether that dealing is through forgiveness, counseling or whatever, that person will hold hatred toward the significant other who cheated or will have fears and insecurities towards others. In other words, he or she will make the life of the significant other hell – as well as make hell the life of anyone else he or she decides to involve him or herself with in the future. When a person cheats on someone to whom they have professed their love, fidelity and partnership to, they are not having fun, they are crying out for help. There is a reason why every action is this world is committed and cheating is no exception. People don't cheat just to cheat. They cheat because there is a problem. The thing, which magnifies the cheating problem, is that very few people actually care to help. They would rather condemn and alienate these individuals as if they were smelly, single sided conversation having, homeless people. Instead of this being a society of 'let's figure out why this person cheats, then let's help him' this society is more 'you cheated, you're scum – you're going to hell, let's kill you!' It's a sad time when the innocent people are just as guilty as the cheaters in relationships.

End

COMMENTS AND OPINIONS ARE ALWAYS
WELCOME – FACEBOOK.COM / JEREMIAH DOTSON
SUPERAUTHOR@HOTMAIL.COM

THE CORRECT WAY TO FOOL AROUND PART 2

www.ingramcontent.com/pod-product-compliance
Lightning Source LLC
Chambersburg PA
CBHW071150290526
45788CB00001BA/296